Cube Based Incremental Data Mining

Ziv Pollak

Cube Based Incremental Data Mining

Using Multi-Dimensional Cubes for Incremental Data Mining

VDM Verlag Dr. Müller

Impressum/Imprint (nur für Deutschland/ only for Germany)

Bibliografische Information der Deutschen Nationalbibliothek: Die Deutsche Nationalbibliothek verzeichnet diese Publikation in der Deutschen Nationalbibliografie; detaillierte bibliografische Daten sind im Internet über http://dnb.d-nb.de abrufbar.

Alle in diesem Buch genannten Marken und Produktnamen unterliegen warenzeichen-, marken- oder patentrechtlichem Schutz bzw. sind Warenzeichen oder eingetragene Warenzeichen der jeweiligen Inhaber. Die Wiedergabe von Marken, Produktnamen, Gebrauchsnamen, Handelsnamen, Warenbezeichnungen u.s.w. in diesem Werk berechtigt auch ohne besondere Kennzeichnung nicht zu der Annahme, dass solche Namen im Sinne der Warenzeichen- und Markenschutzgesetzgebung als frei zu betrachten wären und daher von jedermann benutzt werden dürften.

Coverbild: www.purestockx.com

Verlag: VDM Verlag Dr. Müller Aktiengesellschaft & Co. KG
Dudweiler Landstr. 99, 66123 Saarbrücken, Deutschland
Telefon +49 681 9100-698, Telefax +49 681 9100-988, Email: info@vdm-verlag.de
Zugl.: Tel Aviv, Tel-Aviv University, Israel, PhD Dissertation, 2008

Herstellung in Deutschland:
Schaltungsdienst Lange o.H.G., Berlin
Books on Demand GmbH, Norderstedt
Reha GmbH, Saarbrücken
Amazon Distribution GmbH, Leipzig
ISBN: 978-3-639-13976-1

Imprint (only for USA, GB)

Bibliographic information published by the Deutsche Nationalbibliothek: The Deutsche Nationalbibliothek lists this publication in the Deutsche Nationalbibliografie; detailed bibliographic data are available in the Internet at http://dnb.d-nb.de.

Any brand names and product names mentioned in this book are subject to trademark, brand or patent protection and are trademarks or registered trademarks of their respective holders. The use of brand names, product names, common names, trade names, product descriptions etc. even without a particular marking in this works is in no way to be construed to mean that such names may be regarded as unrestricted in respect of trademark and brand protection legislation and could thus be used by anyone.

Cover image: www.purestockx.com

Publisher:
VDM Verlag Dr. Müller Aktiengesellschaft & Co. KG
Dudweiler Landstr. 99, 66123 Saarbrücken, Germany
Phone +49 681 9100-698, Fax +49 681 9100-988, Email: info@vdm-publishing.com
Tel Aviv, Tel-Aviv University, Israel, PhD Dissertation, 2008

Printed in the U.S.A.
Printed in the U.K. by (see last page)
ISBN: 978-3-639-13976-1

Tel Aviv University

The Faculty of Management

The Leon Recanati Graduate School of Business Administration

Cube Based Incremental Data Mining

Ph.D. Dissertation

Submitted by: Ziv Pollak

Supervisors:

Prof. Israel Spiegler

Prof. Jacob Zahavi

September 2008

List of Figures

List of Tables

Abstract

Data mining models have been getting more popular in recent years, as data mining algorithms and software become widely available and the gathering of new data becomes easier. Data mining models are currently used to support a myriad of applications in a variety of industries. Unfortunately, data mining models built on previous data become obsolete as new data comes in. This work addresses the problem of updating these models in light of new data; referred to as incremental data mining.

Ideally, one could update the data mining models by modifying the existing ones to reflect the incremental data. This could be done by keeping some summary statistics pertaining to the existing model and using them with the new data to update the model. Unfortunately, this approach is only possible in certain models and it is not general enough for all data mining models.

In this work we developed a cube-based approach for incremental data mining that operates on the data, rather than on the data mining algorithms. The idea was to build a compressed replica of the full-blown database by representing the database by means of multi-dimensional cubes, and then applying the original data mining algorithms on the cube-based data. This way, the storage requirement to accommodate the database is not affected by the new data. Yet, the fact that we used the original data mining algorithms on the cube-based data makes our incremental data mining approach very general as it can be applied to all types of data mining models.

To show that our incremental data mining approach is both efficient and accurate, we implemented the cube-based approach on realistic dataset using five different data mining algorithms: linear regression, logistic regression, classification, clustering, and rule induction. In all cases we showed that the results obtained by using the cube-based approach for incremental data mining were very similar to those obtained by applying the original models on the full-blown dataset, and in some cases even better (as it cleaned more noise). In addition, as these algorithms convert the data into cubes in the

8

preprocessing stage, were there is no full visibility of the entire dataset. This work addressed this problem and developed several algorithms to resolve resulting issues.

The cube-based approach has another major advantage in that it uses less than 1% of the storage requirements to accommodate the original dataset. This makes it even more general as it can also be applied to building models on the original database and not just for incremental data mining.

1 Introduction

1.1 Incremental data mining

The information age in which we live is characterized by an enormous amount of data of different types. There is too much data and not enough information. This is a problem which afflicts most companies and organizations today. The solution to this problem lies with knowledge discovery (data mining) as this can extract the information hidden within the data and use it for decision making [1,2,3,4,5].

A crucial problem with data mining is updating the knowledge as new data becomes available. And in today's dynamic world, new data arrives even as we speak. There are three ways to handle this new data: First, one can ignore it and still use the old knowledge. While this saves computation time, decisions based on obsolete knowledge might be incorrect. Another possibility is to recreate the knowledge by running the knowledge discovery process on the entire dataset, including both the old and the new data. While this will keep the knowledge up-to-date, the computational burden may be prohibitive. A third option is to use an incremental approach which begins with the existing knowledge and updates it to reflect the new set of observations. Depending upon the application, the updating procedure could be done in a batch mode, or in an online mode.

This incremental approach has a few major benefits:
- **The knowledge is always kept up-to-date** – Incrementally updating the knowledge keeps it current and ready to be used for decision-support.
- **Saving processing resources and time** - Rebuilding knowledge from scratch may require a great deal of processing time and resources. Using an incremental approach to update it makes the procedure much more efficient.
- **Update speed** – For those applications where response time is critical (e.g. fraud), the incremental approach to updating knowledge may be the only alternative to keeping it

current. Data processing is often the most expensive component of the knowledge discovery process. Incremental algorithms, by definition, process far less data and are therefore faster.

- **Service level** – At the time knowledge is updated, the service level of the system might be affected, as it still uses old rules and patterns. Thus, one needs to decrease the time taken to update the knowledge as much as possible. This is only possible with incremental algorithms.

- **Saving the data is not needed** – Non-incremental algorithms for updating knowledge often require storing all the data so that when new observations come in, the model can be rebuilt on the entire dataset to update the knowledge. Incremental algorithms do not require re-scanning of data that has already been processed and thus results in enormous savings in both storage space and processing times. This issue is especially critical in applications where large volumes of data are involved.

1.2 Problem statement

Incremental algorithms require that one keep a summary of the processed data. This summary is used in combination with the new data to ensure an accurate model update whenever new data arrives.

The major problem with the data summary is to clearly define what needs to be saved in it. This summary must be:

- **Useful** - The summary must contain all the information needed in order to update the model in the best possible way.

- **Detailed** - The summary must be detailed enough to allow even for the most complex knowledge update. For example, in a clustering problem we may need to split an existing cluster of data points into two separate clusters. In this case we need enough details in order to determine the size and location of these two new clusters. Practically this means that we must retain all the data points in this cluster.

- **Limited memory** - The summary should be stored in memory while the analytical

11

approach algorithm processes the new samples. Therefore, the amount of memory needed to store it must be as limited as possible. Ideally, the size of the summary should be independent of the volume of data involved and remain fixed even if additional data is available.

- **Minimal effect on the data processing rate** – In those cases in which the rate of processing data in a critical element in the system (e.g., in online processing), the updating procedure of the summary must be fast enough in order not to slow down the processing rate.

Previous work has shown that one can find the needed summary information for specific data mining algorithms (see the next section for examples and details). By analyzing the way the algorithm works and the data it processes, one can sometimes yield this summarized information and save it as part of the algorithm's operation. This approach is limited as doing this analysis and coming up with the actual needed summary is not possible in all cases - there are many situations where finding those summary statistics is not possible, or requires saving the entire data set.

This work comes to resolve this problem of finding the specific summary statistics for each algorithm by developing a generic approach to save summarized data which can be used for every incremental data mining algorithm.

The approach described in this work is unique as it works on the data, rather than on the algorithm or the model. It is an alternative method of representing data, which has been borrowed from the data abstraction and the On-Line Analytical Processing OLAP field [65, 66, 67, 68]. Instead of trying to store the internal parameters of the algorithm (which requires a new set of parameters for each algorithm), we use a "meta-data" approach for representing the data. In this approach the data is summarized in a fairly aggregated format, yet with enough details to ensure that accuracy is not overly sacrificed.

1.3 Contribution

This work developed a way to use multi-dimensional histograms (cubes) to abstract data and allow us to save a summarized, yet detailed version of the data. These cubes are then used by incremental data mining algorithms in order to accurately update the model whenever new data arrives.

This work has several major novelties and contributions:
The use of cubes for incremental data mining. Previous work has been undertaken on the topic of summarizing data into cubes for data mining and on the topic of incremental data mining. The novelty of this work is the combination of these two fields and the use of cubes for incremental data mining.

The main work in the area of summarizing data into cubes for data mining includes: MedGen [93] which is cube based version of the well known C4.5 [132] algorithms, CLIQUE [96] which uses cubes to find high density areas for clustering, [94] which describe cube based association rules mining algorithms, based on the Apriori method [82]. Additional algorithms and the summaries data for data mining are described in the literature review chapter (section 2.2).

A different research area which has recently made lots of progress is incremental data mining. The most well known examples are: ID4 [14] which is an incremental version of ID3 [12], CLS [15] which addresses the issue of incremental classification, the incremental clustering algorithm HIERARCH [25], the incremental tree induction algorithm (ITI) [85], Kalles' algorithm for tree induction [86] and incremental rule induction [176]. Additional incremental data mining algorithms are described in the literature review (section 2.1). These papers describe incremental data mining algorithms and are not concerned with the way data should be efficiently saved for those algorithms.

The unique contribution of this work is that cubes are used in order to save the needed summarized data to perform incremental knowledge updates. The cubes described in this work allow saving a summary of the previously processed data and at the same time holding enough detail to ensure correct incremental model update. Therefore, this work takes the best of both worlds and "combines" them into creating cubes that summarize the data for incremental data mining.

Second, this work also describes a generic solution to the problem of data summarization. All the algorithms described above (and in the literature review section) are aimed at solving a specific summarization problem/algorithm. This work describes a generic approach that can be used in every data mining algorithms, no matter what model it is building (regression, clustering, classification, rules induction, etc.). In our case, we focused the solution of summarizing the data around the representation of the data and its distribution in the problem's space. This allowed us to create a generic solution that can be used for any algorithm. This work describes the generic approach to summarize the data, and then implements it on different data mining algorithms to prove its usability and accuracy.

The generic way in which the data is summarized saves the need to develop new ways of summarizing the data when new algorithms are developed. This approach can be used for all incremental data mining algorithms. In addition, it allows us to summarize one dataset, and then use it for multiple algorithms at the same time (without the need to create different summaries for different algorithms). An example of where this attribute is useful is a bank. The customers data can be summarized and then used for both classification and clustering using the same generic summary of the data.

Third, the cubes introduced here allow the saving of memory and computational resources for data mining algorithms. This shows that when using the cubes, and not the original data, less than 1% of the original amount of memory is required, and there is also a considerable saving in the required computational resources for updating the knowledge. This means that the developed cube model can be used for any data mining algorithm in order to save storage space and computational resources.

14

Fourth, in order for any data mining algorithm to create a correct model, the data used by the algorithm must be pre-processed. As this work addresses the issues of using cubes data for incremental algorithm, it has also contributed to the development of various pre-processing procedures that allow the handling of specific problems that can occur with pre-processing data which is going to be stored in cubes. For example, accommodation of new data points which are not represented in the existing cubes (e.g., a data point with extreme attribute values).

1.4 Research Plan
This work focuses on using aggregated data for incremental data mining. The research plan for this work is as follows:

- Devising the cube-based approach for representing data for incremental algorithms which is based on splitting the data space into several multi-dimensional histograms.
- Developing an incremental algorithm for updating knowledge, and utilizing the cube-based approach for data representation, for each of the five major model classes in data mining – linear regression, logistic regression, classification, clustering and rule induction. In cases where there are multiple algorithms per model class (i.e., classification), we have selected one algorithm (e.g., CHAID [11]) to develop the analytical and the cube-based equivalents.
- Applying the non-incremental data mining algorithms and the cube-based incremental algorithms on realistic dataset; a non-profit dataset provided by the DMEF (The Direct Marketing Educational Foundation).
  In order to check the stability and overfitting of the algorithms, all models were built from a *training set* and then validated on an independent *validation set* (holdout sample). For the non-incremental algorithm, the dataset was split into two mutually exclusive sets; the training dataset and the validation dataset. For the incremental algorithms, both the analytical and the cube-based, the database was split into three mutually exclusive datasets: a training dataset used to create the initial model; an incremental dataset used to incrementally update the knowledge; and a validation dataset used to evaluate the model results.

15

- Evaluating the results by comparing the knowledge obtained from the incremental cube-based approach to the knowledge obtained by the non incremental algorithms on the entire dataset. The performance criteria used to evaluate the models varied by the type of model class involved and is discussed separately in each of the implementation chapters (8-12) below.

1.5 Research method

This work can be divided into two major parts each has its own research method. The first introduces the cube model and uses simulations to show how it is used along with its major benefits. The second part describes the implementation of the cube-based approach on different types of data mining algorithms.

The first part of the work starts with a theoretical explanation of the need for the cube model. It continues with introducing the cube-based approach and shows how it can be used to represent the original data. Then it describes how cube-based approach is used and the major benefits of the cube model to save memory and handle noisy data. Simulated examples are used though out the entire first part of the work in order to demonstrate specific points and allow easier understanding.

The second part of the work, describes the implementation of the cubes based approach on five different types of data mining algorithms. This section starts with describing the "real life" database which was used in this work (the DMEF non profit database), and later describes the different algorithms which were implemented using the cube approach: linear regression, logistic regression, classification, clustering and rule induction.

For each one of the algorithms we start with a short discussion on the way the algorithm performance should be evaluated (both the non-incremental and the incremental algorithms are evaluated using the same criteria), describe the original and the cube-based incremental algorithms and then compare the results of running both algorithms on the database. We analyze the results of the cube-based incremental algorithm and

16

compare them to the original algorithms' results. In these sections, we compare actual implementation results (actual data mining algorithms and "real life" database) in order to validate the contribution of the cube-based model when it is used for incremental data mining.

This work shows that using the cube-based approach for incremental data mining is a good alternative to the existing algorithms. The results produced by the new algorithms were as good as (if not better) then the original algorithms. In addition, we show that the cube based approach has additional benefits such as a saving of storage space and reduced amount of computation resources needed.

1.6 Organization of this Work

Section 2 provides a literature review of the topics related to this work. Section 3 describes the theoretical aspects of the model utilized in this work, including dimensionality and noise reduction. Section 4 describes the cube-based model and its use and Section 5 discusses the important data pre-processing issue for incremental computations. This is followed by describing the dataset used in this work in Section 6. The next sections describe the developed cube-based incremental algorithms: linear regression (Section 7), logistic regression (Section 8), classification (Section 9), clustering (Section 10) and association rules induction (Section 11). Section 12 concludes the work with a short summary.

2 Literature Review

This work addresses the topic of cube based of incremental data mining algorithms. In order to fully understand the problem and its context this chapter reviews the main literature in both the field data mining and cube based algorithms.

In more details, this chapter reviews the following research fields:

- Data mining – Data mining algorithms produce knowledge. This section will review and main incremental and non-incremental data mining algorithms.
- Multi-dimensional histogram ("cubes") - the solution to the incremental data mining problem described in this work is based on multi-dimensional histograms. In this section the multi-dimensional histograms will be explained and existing algorithms that uses multi-dimensional histograms will be reviewed.
- OLAP – the use of multi-dimensional histogram in this work is similar to the OLAP "summary" solution. This section reviews some of the OLAP methods and clarifies the difference between the data-warehouse cube and the cubes described in this work.

2.1 Data Mining

Data Mining [1] is a research field whose goal is to produce "useful conclusions", called knowledge, from large amounts of data (or information). This field was created due to the large amounts of data found in databases and the desire to make them useful.

Data mining is used in many fields, for example:

- Marketing - Trying to predict the next purchase by a customer or to recommend to him a product that he is likely to buy.
- Investments - Trying to predict good investments based on historical data.
- Communication - fraud detection

Data mining algorithms create knowledge which can be presented in many different formats [1, 8]. The most common formats are:

18

- Regression - predicting the value of a given variable holding other variables constant. For example: Predicting the chance a patient will be sick, given the results of several medical tests, or predicting the demand for a product given its level of publicity.
- Classification - Splitting data into pre-defined groups. For example: splitting the bank customers between those who can own a credit card and those who do not.
- Clustering - Splitting the data into groups (not pre-defined). For example: finding a similar population of buyers from a specific store.
- Association Rules - describe the knowledge in form of rule "if <condition> then <result>".

These forms of representing knowledge are not mutually exclusive, for example: association rules can represent groups created by classification algorithms. This chapter will review the main algorithms (both incremental and non-incremental) for each one of these forms.

2.1.1 Regression

Regression is aimed to predict the value of a dependent variable (or target) given the independent variables values. Another way to describe the problem is to understand the relationship between several independent variables and a dependent variable.

The most common regression model used is linear regression [9]. The linear regression model finds a linear correlation between the dependent variables and the independent variables (assuming any exist). This relationship is evaluated using the least squares criteria [9] - by solving a set of equations on these parameters. A straight line relationship can be valuable in summarizing the observed dependence of one variable or another. The method in which this line can be created is described in detail in the following chapter, and will therefore not be described here.

One of the main parameters in order to evaluate the quality of the regression line is the R^2 parameter. R^2 defined as [9]:

$$R^2 = \frac{SS\_due\_to\_regression}{Total\_SS} = \frac{SSR}{SST}$$

Where

$$SSR = \sum_{i=1}^{n}(\hat{Y}_i - \overline{Y})^2$$

$$SST = \sum_{i=1}^{n}(Y_i - \overline{Y})^2$$

Y_i are the actual data points

$\overline{Y}$ is the average Y value

$\hat{Y}_i$ are the predicted Y values based on the regression line

The R^2 measures the "portion of total variation about the mean $\overline{Y}$ explained by the regression", and therefore can be used as one of the parameters in order to evaluate the quality of the created regression model.

Another well known regression model is logistic regression [10]. In this case, the dependent variable is a binary and can have only two possible values 0 or 1. The algorithm to calculate the logistic regression is described in details in the following chapters.

The difference between the logistic regression model and the linear regression model is that the outcome variable in logistic regression is binary or dichotomous. This difference is reflected both in the choice of parametric model and in the assumptions taken when the model is created. Once the difference are accounted for, the methods employed in an analysis using logistic regression follow the same general principles used in linear regression. Thus, the techniques used in linear regression analysis are the motivation for the logistic regression analysis [10].

To conclude, regression analysis is a very useful tool in the data mining and statistical analysis. There are many different existing algorithms to build these models, but there are no incremental algorithms to build a regression model. In this work a generic incremental regression algorithm will be developed.

2.1.2 Classification

Classification is a way to describe knowledge in cases where each sample needs to be categorized into one of several pre-defined groups based on the sample attributes.

The classification decision mechanism can be presented in several forms; one of the most common being classification trees. In this case, decision trees are created where the leaves contain the name of the group to which the samples belong and the nodes contain decisions based on the values of the attributes. The goal in the creation of decision trees is to place the most important attributes closest to the tree's root, to ensure that the resultant tree will be smaller and more generic, thereby increasing the chance to correctly classify new samples.

One of the most well known algorithms for building of decision trees is CHAID[11]. The algorithm creates a decision tree where the decision in the nodes is based on chi-square tests.
Another algorithm for the creation of decision trees is ID3 [12]. This algorithm is based on entropy [13] to decide which attribute to choose at each level. The incremental version of ID3 is known as ID4 [14] and is known as one of the first attempts to handle the problem of incremental tree construction.

Another attempt to handle the problem of incremental classification is the CLS [15] algorithm. CLS sets the order of the nodes based on counting the number of appearances of each attribute and finding the attribute that best describes how the data is divided into groups. The CLS algorithm is significant since it shows that changes in the classification mechanism are needed only when new samples are classified incorrectly (and therefore no changes are required for new samples that are correctly classified).
This research direction continues to evolve in [16] studies that limit the use of samples in the learning process. The next step in incremental classification research was the adaptation of AQ [17]. In this case the algorithm can re-build the knowledge based only on number of new samples and there is no need to use all the samples for knowledge re-building. This makes the knowledge re-building process much faster and more efficient.

A subsequent step in this research field was the GEM algorithm [18] that is capable of fixing the errors in knowledge, without requiring a complete re-build of the knowledge base.

A different approach to classification is "nearest neighbor" [19]. In this method the classification of a sample is based on finding the most similar sample and setting the classification according to the existing sample. There are cases in which more than one existing sample can be used to classify the new sample. The advantage of this approach is its simplicity, while the disadvantage is that for each new sample all the existing samples need to be scanned. There is no actual knowledge representation in this case.

There are a variety of classification algorithms both incremental and non-incremental and this work presents a generic basis for the creation of incremental algorithms, and subsequently presents an incremental classification algorithm created on this basis.

2.1.3 Clustering

Clustering is a way to present knowledge in cases where each sample needs to be categorized into one of several non-pre-defined groups based on the sample attributes. The clustering problem is known as an unsupervised learning problem, since there is no definition of the groups, and the algorithm need to find the groups on its own without the benefit of any supervision. There are cases in which the number of the groups is limited in advance (by the user) so as not to create too many groups by the clustering algorithm. The algorithms that handle the clustering problem can be divided into two types:

- Division algorithms - These algorithms start from one large group that contain all the data and split it into smaller groups. For example: CLARANS [20].
- Hierarchical algorithms - These algorithms try to unite similar samples into one group, and then similar groups into larger groups. For example: CURE [21].

Many clustering algorithms have been developed, a good review of the major ones can be found in [22]. This section reviews the main clustering algorithms that are relevant for this work.

22

EPAM [23] is known as one of the earliest algorithms for concept formation. The algorithm was designed as a physiological model to try and understand the human learning in cases of verbal memory. Based on EPAM the algorithm UNIMEM [7] was developed. UNIMEM uses hill-climbing search method in order to form the groups and create hierarchy. Hamming distance is used to measure the similarity between the groups, and the center of each group (cluster centroid) is used to describe it.

Another algorithm that uses the hill-climbing search method is COBWEB [6]. This algorithm builds hierarchies of mutually exclusive groups where the leaves of the hierarchy are the data samples. The limitation of the COBWEB algorithm is that each group is expressed in terms of normal distribution (average and standard deviation). The CURE algorithm [21] attempts to overcome this limitation by forming groups of different form and size. The CURE algorithm describes each group by using a fixed number of points which are selected from within the group. By using more then just one point to represent the group the algorithm has the ability to represent groups in many different ways. Another advantage the CURE method has is its ability to handle large databases, due to its ability to split and sample the dataset. The process starts with splitting the data in the dataset into sets, and then to sample each set. The clustering is performed on these samples.

Another algorithm to cluster large data sets is BIRCH [24]. The algorithm uses the attributes that describe the natural closeness of the data in order to divide them into groups. These attributes are saved and then updated incrementally using a CF-tree.

Another incremental clustering algorithm is HIERARCH [25]. The algorithm uses two modules in order to handle new samples presented to it: one module to simplify the sample for generalization and the other uses the results from the first module to perform an iterative branch and bound process in order to find the optimum combination of the generalized sample in the existing knowledge.

A different approach to clustering is taken by the well known K-means clustering algorithm [26]. This algorithm starts by randomly creating the needed clusters and then updating them iteratively in order to create the best clusters possible.

Again we see that though there is a large variety of clustering algorithms to handle different problems, the number of incremental clustering algorithms is very small. The algorithms that can be regarded as incremental clustering algorithms are COBWEB, UNIMEM and HIERARCH. This work attempts to reduce the gap between the great need for incremental algorithms and the complexity of creating them both by describing a generic method to store the algorithm's internal parameters and by describing new incremental algorithms.

2.1.4 Rule Induction

Rules are a different format to represent knowledge. In case of rules the knowledge is presented in the form of "If *(x)* Then *(y)*.". A well known algorithm to determine rules is Apriori [27]. The Apriori algorithm starts by finding the most common itemsets in the database, and then uses the common itemsets in order to create association rules.

Another rules algorithm is AQ [17]. The process of creating rules in AQ is an iterative process. In each stage, a rule is created (as general as possible), and the samples described by this rules are deleted. The process repeats itself until there are no samples that were not deleted. Additionally, AQ can perform this task incrementally [28]. For each new sample, if there are rules that contradict the sample they are deleted and the algorithm is activated again to create new rules for the samples that are not being described by any rule.

An alternate algorithm to find rules is CN2 [29]. This algorithm combines the effectiveness of handling noise with the ability to create rules. CN2 is an adaptation of the AQ [17] algorithms so there will be no dependency in samples using the search, thus enlarging the search space. One of the differences between CN2 and AQ, is that the set of rules received from CN2 is ordered and the rules must be activated according to their order.

Another algorithm that creates rules by abstracting of the data is [87]. The algorithm summarizes the data using hierarchies and then finds patterns on those hierarchies.

Mining of association rules from large data sets has been focused topic in recent data mining research [82, 110, 111, 112, 113, 114, 115, 116, 117, 118, 119, 120, 121, 122, 123, 124, 125, 126], but the still could only find once example of incremental algorithm for rule induction [115]. This clearly shows (once again), that the number of existing incremental knowledge update algorithms is very limited.

The research field of data mining is very broad. There are different ways to represent knowledge and different algorithms to produce this knowledge. The data mining field has mainly treated the problem of creating the knowledge and there is little reference to the problem of incrementally updating the knowledge. This work serves to further explore the problem of incremental knowledge update as well as describe a generic method that assists in the creation of new incremental algorithms as well as creates several new incremental algorithms to update knowledge.

2.2 Multidimensional Histograms

2.2.1 What are cubes ?

Histograms are a way to represent the distribution of a variable in a space efficient manner [31]. They have been design to work well for numeric value domains, and have many uses, mainly in the field of databases, for example, support cost-based query optimization [32-43], approximate query answering [44 - 49], data mining for time series data [50] and map simplification [51].

A histogram on an attribute X is constructed by using a partitioning rule to partition its data distribution into B (where B>1) where mutually disjointed subsets called buckets approximate the frequencies and values in each bucket in some common fashion [42]. Good histograms partition data sets into "smooth" buckets with close-to-uniform internal tuple density. In other words, the frequency variance of the tuples enclosed in a bucket is minimized, leading to accurate selection estimations for range queries.

A partition of a multi-dimensional data domain results in a set of disjointed rectangular buckets that cover all the points in the domain and assigns to each bucket some aggregated information, usually the number of tuples enclosed. The choice of rectangular buckets is justified by two key factors: First, rectangular buckets make it easy and efficient to intersect each bucket and a given range query to estimate selectivity. Second, rectangular buckets can be represented concisely, which allows a large number of buckets to be stored using the given budget constraints [40] describes the taxonomy of partitioning schemas for building multi-dimensional histograms.

A variety of problems require succinct summary representations of large data sets. Histograms are an important example of such summary representation structures [40].

2.2.2 Using cubes in data mining algorithms

With the development of the cubes model to store data there have been numerous studies on cube based data mining. This section will review the major ones.

Classification using cubes

In order to create an efficient and scalable algorithm for classification of large database a preliminary step has been added to the conventional classification algorithms (like C4.5 [132]) – Generalization by attribute oriented induction. In this step, the generalized data is stored in a multi-dimensional data cubes to allow fast accessing. Applying attribute-oriented induction prior to classification substantially reduces the computational complexity of this data intensive process [129]. Data can be compressed with a concept tree ascension technique which replaces attributes values by generalized concept from corresponding attribute concept hierarchies [127]. Concept hierarchies may be provided by domain experts or database administrators, or may be defined using the database schema [127]. Concept hierarchies for numeric attributes can be generated automatically [128].

One of the most known algorithms for cube based classification is the MedGen Algorithm [93] which is a slightly modified version of the C4.5 [132] classification algorithm. The algorithm first generalizes the data to cubes, then apply relevance analysis, and later apply the same algorithm as C4.5.

Clustering using cubes

A data point typically has dozens of attributes and the domain for each attribute can be large. It is not meaningful to look for clusters in such high dimensional space as the average density of point anywhere in the data space is likely to be quite low [130]. Compounding this problem, many dimensions can have noise or values which are uniformly distributed. Therefore distance functions that use all the dimensions of the data may be ineffective.

Several ways has been proposed to over come this problem, for example [131]. A different approach is density based approach. In this case, the problem is to automatically identify projections of the input data into a subset of attributes with the property that these projections include regions of high density [96]. To approximate the density of the data points, the data space has been partitioned into cubes and the number of data samples in each cube was indicated. Once the appropriate cubes were found the task is to find clusters in the corresponding projections. One algorithm that achieves this is described in [96]

Association Rules using cubes

[94] describes a Multi-D-Slicing algorithm, which finds a large 1-predicate sets in p (where p is the number of predicates in a given meta-rules). This algorithm adopts the spirit of table-based approach to association rules mining, such as Apriori [82] but uses a cube structure instead of the original data.

To sum, we can see that in several cases the cube based mining inherited the spirit of relation or transactional data mining methods, such as [82,97]. Further discussion of issues related to efficient and effective data mining in large data warehouses can be found in [91].

2.2.3 Other cube based algorithms

Multi-dimensional cubes have been used in many different algorithms in order to store a summary of the data. One of the leading researches in this field is Jiawei Han who had developed (with a team of researches and students) several interesting cube based algorithms:

- CubeExplorer is an integrated environment for online exploration of data cubes [89]
- P-cube [90] is an algorithm to create data cube specifically for preference queries in multi dimensional space
- [98] which discuss the topic of building cubes from spatial data.
- Ranking cubes is a computational model developed for answering k-top queries using multi-dimensional cubes [99]
- [92] describe a cube based concept description
- [95] describe a cube based prediction algorithms.
- Cubes have been also used in order to analyze access patterns in web logs. The algorithms describe in [100] aggregate the page hit counts of web pages into cubes and then find patterns using these cubes.
- An cube based approach has been also developed for meta-rule-guided mining (which is an interactive approach to data mining), where users probe the data under analysis by specifying hypotheses in form of meta-rules or pattern templates [101].

It is often too expensive to compute all the high-dimensional data cubes. Therefore, additional research has been done on ways to reduce the amount of memory to store the cubes. Few examples are: [106] which describe a method to find summaries of the data cubes, [107,108, 109] who address the issue of cube compression, [104, 105] that Are computing iceberg cube, which contains only aggregates above certain thresholds.

All the algorithms described above store summarized data into cubes and then use the cubes for specific need. The approach presented in this work is different in two ways: First, the cubes are used for incremental data mining. Reviewing the exiting literature we

29

have not found any mention to using cubes for incremental data mining. This work shows that using cubes for data mining has several benefits and can achieve very good results. Second, while each of the algorithms above solve a specific need to store data in cubes, this work aim to describe a generic approach that is suitable to handle any data mining algorithm and not just a specific algorithm. This prevents the need to develop a new approach for each data mining algorithm and therefore it is very efficient.

2.2.4 Use of Histograms in Databases

The most common use of histograms in databases is for selectivity estimation during query optimization [52]. Most database management systems (DBMS's) maintain a variety of statistics on the content of the database in order to estimate various quantities, such as selectives within cost-based query optimizer [46]. The most common technique used in practice for selectivity estimation is maintaining histograms on the frequency distribution of an attribute. A histogram groups attribute values into "buckets" (subsets) and approximate true attributes values and their frequencies based on summary statistics maintained in a bucket [53].

Histograms are used to estimate the cost of physical database operators in a query plan. The results of such estimations through the use of a histogram represents the approximate number of tuples satisfying the selective estimate and can determine whether a database index should be used to execute this operation.

Histograms have also been used in approximate query answering systems, where the main objective is to provide a quick but approximate answer to a user query, providing error guarantees. Research has been conducted on the construction of histograms for this task [44,46]. Multi-dimensional histograms can be an effective tool for accurate multi-attribute query selectivity estimation [54]

An example of the need for histograms in query estimation is: Assume that the database contains information for 2500 companies and for each company we have a record with its financial information for each of the past 20 years, a total of 50,000 tuples. When the query "find all the tuples in which sales > 20 M$ and the year = 1977" is analyzed it seems like there are two possible ways to perform this query: First, using the sale attribute – scan all the tuples and find those with sale > 20 M$, then for each tuple check if the year is 1977. Second, using the year attribute – scan all the tuples and find those with year = 1977, then for each tuple check if sales > 20M$. The decision which option to chose should be based on the amount of tuples in which the year = 1977 and the amount of tuples in which sale >20M$ - the one that return less tuples should be used. In order to estimate which sub query will return the fewest tuples an histogram can be used.

Another use of histograms in DBMSs is for approximate query processing [55,47] to give rough and fast responses to expensive queries [56]. Since the histogram represents an approximation of the distribution of the data over an attribute, this distribution can be used in order to give a rough answer to a query.

A third use of histograms is based on the fact the histograms are a concise and flexible way to construct summary structures for large data sets. This enables the use of histogram as a basic tool for data visualization and analysis [56].

Fourth, in the past most commercial DBMS's were based on the "attribute value independence assumption". Under this assumption, the data distributions of individual attributes in a relation are independent of each other [42]. This assumption helped to simplify the processing needed in the database, but it is seldom correct. An alternative to assuming attribute value independence is to use histograms over multiple attributes, which are generally referred to as multi-dimensional histograms [39,42]. Nowadays, one-dimensional histograms have now been adopted by several commercial database systems (e.g. DB2, Informix, Oracle, Microsoft, and Sybase) replacing the native and rarely valid uniformity assumption [57].

Due to these uses, histogram based techniques for approximation of one-dimensional data distribution has been extensively studied in the research literature [57,43]. These studies have led to finding other fields in which histograms can be useful.

31

2.3 OLAP

The relational data model, which was introduced by E.F. Codd in 1970 [58], served as the foundation of today's database industry. During the past decade, the multidimensional data model emerged for use when the objective is to analyze data rather than to perform online transactions [103,59]. Multidimensional data models have three important application areas within data analysis:

- Data warehouses – large repositories that integrate data from several sources
- Online analysis processing (OLAP) – systems provide fast answers for queries that aggregate large amount of detailed data
- Data mining – Applications that seek to discover knowledge by searching for unknown patterns and relationships.

Essentially, OLAP analysis takes a snapshot of a relational database and restructures it into dimensional data. An OLAP structure created from the data is called an OLAP cube. The OLAP cube is divided into cells where each cell contains an aggregation of relational data. The number of possible aggregations is determined by every possible manner in which the original data can be hierarchically linked.

A good definition of the term OLAP is found in [60]: "… On-Line Analytical Processing (OLAP) is a category of software technology that enables analysts, managers and executives to gain insight into data through fast, consistent, interactive access to a wide variety of possible views of information that has been transformed from raw data to reflect the real dimensionality of the enterprise as understood by the user".
The focus of OLAP tools is to provide multidimensional analysis of the underlying information. To achieve this goal, these tools employ multidimensional models for the storage and presentation of data. Data are organized in cubes (or hypercubes), which are defined over a multidimensional space, consisting of several dimensions.

2.3.1 OLAP Models

The *data cube* operator was introduced in [61]. This operator expands a relational table, by computing the aggregations over all the possible subspaces created from the combinations of the attributes of such a relation. Practically, the cube operator calculates all the marginal aggregations of the detailed data set. In [62] a multidimensional data model is introduced based on the relational elements. Dimensions are modeled as *dimension relations*, practically annotating attributes with dimension names.

In [63] Gyssens and Lakshmanan define *n-dimensional* tables and a relational mapping through the notion of *completion*. Algebra is defined with classical relational operators as well as restructuring, classification and summarization operators. In [64] the relational model is extended and a new language is proposed.

2.3.2 Cube-Oriented Models

The OLAP research field contains several efforts to model the multidimensional databases directly and more naturally. In [65] a model for multidimensional databases is described, which is characterized from its symmetric treatment of dimensions and measures. A set of operators is also introduced dealing with the construction and destruction of cubes. In addition, [66] describes a way to model a multidimensional database through the notion of *dimensions* and *f-tables*. Dimensions are constructed from hierarchies of the dimension level, whereas f-tables are repositories of the factual data. In [67] dimensions and dimension hierarchies are explicitly modeled. Furthermore, an algebra representing the common OLAP operations is provided. The model is based on the concept of the *basic cube* representing the cube with the model's detailed information, where all other cubes are calculated as expressions overlaid on the basic cubes.

Lehner represents another model based on primary and secondary multidimensional objects in [68]. A Primary Multidimensional Object, which represents a cube, consists of: a cell identifier, a schema definition, a set of selections, an aggregation type (e.g. sum, average, etc.) and a result type. A secondary Multidimensional Object consists of all the dimension levels to which on can roll-up or drill-down for a specific schema. Operations like Roll-up, Drill-down, Slice, Dice etc. are also presented. In [69] which is a sequel to the previous paper, two multidimensional normal forms are proposed, defining the modeling constraints for summary attributes and the constraints to model complex dimensional structures.

DBMiner [88] is one of the most known tools which has been developed in order to run interactive data mining algorithms on OLAP DB. The work is focused on the integration of data mining and OLAP technologies and the development of scalable, integrated and multiple data mining functions.

Data cubes have been playing an essential role in fast OLAP. However, when there is a high number of dimensions (e.g. over 100) and moderate side (e.g. around 106 tuples), no feasible data cube can be constructed. [102] propose a new method called shell-fragment. It vertically partitions a high dimensional data set into a set of disjoint low dimensional datasets called fragments. For each fragment, we compute its local data cube.

2.3.3 The Multi-Dimensional Histograms and OLAP

There is much similarity between the multi-dimensional histogram and the OLAP model. In both cases the original data is summarized into buckets to allow faster processing of the data. Instead of processing the actual data (in queries or in data analysis) the summarized data is used, thus enabling us produce the resulted answer / model with much less processing time.

The term *cube* used in the OLAP terminology to show that data can be perceived as being stored in the cell of a multi-dimensional array or hypercube [30], thus another element of similarity between these two models.

But there is a difference between these two models. In the case of multi-dimensional histograms, the histograms describe the problem's space and the data stored in each one of them are the data points which reside inside this part of the problem's space. In the OLAP model, the cube summarizes data from several different aspects (none of which is

35

related to their position in the problem's space).

The similarity between the multi-dimensional histogram model and the OLAP model is one of the basis elements to this work. This work describes a model in which the multi-dimensional histograms are used to store information for incremental algorithm in a way similar to the way the OLAP cubes is used to store information for OLAP analysis.

3 The Theoretical Aspects of Dimensionality Reduction

3.1 Introduction

One of the major issues that need to be addressed by any data mining algorithm is the large number of dimensions in real life datasets. This chapter will describe the theoretical model behind the dimensionality reducing in those data sets, which will serve as the basis of the cube approach for data representation. We also describe a theoretical model for reducing noise in real life datasets. This model will allow us to demonstrate the advantages of using the cube approach later in this work.

3.2 Reducing the Number of Dimensions

3.2.1 Geometrical Aspects

Also referred to as the "curse of dimensionality" [70], the dimensionality issue, known for more than three decades, has implications in many different fields such as optimization, statistics, etc. We can conceive of high dimensional spaces as extension of low dimensional spaces. For example, a circle in a two-dimensional space is a geometrical form with all points having a fixed distance (radius) from the center. In three dimensional space, this rule creates a sphere. The equivalent of a sphere in the multi dimensional space is the hypersphere. Similarly, in a two-dimensional space, a square is a geometrical shape with four equal sides. The equivalent to a square in a three-dimensional space is the cube and in multi-dimensional space – the hypercube.

By and large, our understanding of multi-dimensional data is often based on our experience with three dimensional Euclidian spaces. But there are many assumptions that apply to low dimensional space that do not extend to multi dimensional spaces. Multi dimensional spaces are too complex to comprehend.

The relation between hyperspheres and hypercubes is given by the following theorem [71]:

Theorem: The volume of the hypersphere of radius r and dimension d is given by the equation:

$$V_s(n) = \frac{\pi^{\frac{n}{2}} * r^n}{\Gamma\left(\frac{n}{2}+1\right)}$$

When Γ is the gamma function $\Gamma(n) = (n-1)!$

The volume of a hypercube in $[-r,r]^d$ is given by the equation:

$$V_s(r) = (2r)^d$$

The fraction of the volume of the hypersphere inscribed in a hypercube is:

$$f = \frac{V_s(r)}{V_c(r)} = \frac{\pi^{\frac{d}{2}}}{d * 2^{d-1} * \Gamma\left(\frac{d}{2}\right)}$$

The figure below shows how f decreases as the dimensionality d increases.

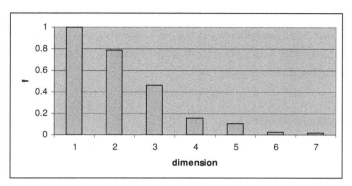

Figure 1 : Relation between f values and the number dimensions

In particular, $\lim_{d \to \infty} f = 0$, which implies that as d increases, the volume of the hypersphere inscribed in a hypercube decreases to 0, e.g. the volume of the hypercube is increasingly concentrated in the corners.

Datasets with d attributes (features) constitute an hypercube with d dimensions in a multidimensional space. The above behavior (which is difficult to understand when thinking in three dimensions only) implies that multi-dimensional data is very sparse. This has two practical implications: First, the volume of the hypercube for a dataset is much smaller than the volume of the corresponding d-dimensional hypersphere. Second, high dimensional observations can be projected to a lower dimension without losing significant information.

But by how much can one reduce dimensionality and still be able to accommodate the data? We deal with this issue below.

3.2.2 Effective Hypercube Dimension for Accommodating a Dataset

Fortunately, in real-life cases, data is not uniformly distributed in the problem space, and as a result one can get by with a much lower dimension space to accommodate the data.

We use the concepts discussed above to find the effective hypercube required to accommodate the data and show that it has a much lower dimension than the dimension of the original problem space. We demonstrate this property by means of several hypothetical, but realistic examples [71].

3.2.2.1 Binary Variables

We start with the case of a dataset which consists only of d binary attributes, each constitutes a dimension. Theoretically the dimension of the hypercube required to represent the dataset in this case is 2^d. This is much too much for the large datasets encountered in data mining applications which often contain large number of dimensions. For example, when d=300, then $2^d=2*10^{90}$.

Theorem 1

Given that the problem space contains d dimensions which are all binary, the Euclidean distance to the origin, $R = \sum_{i=1}^{d} x_i^2$, is approximately normally distributed [71]

Proof:

Using simple probability rules, the probability P(R=r) is given by:

$P(R=0) = P(\text{all the attribute values are "0"}) = 1 / 2^d$

$P(R=1) = P(\text{one attribute value is "1" and all the others are "0"}) = \binom{d}{1} / 2^d$

$P(R=2) = P(\text{two attribute values are "1" and all the others are "0"}) = \binom{d}{2} / 2^d$

...

$P(R = d/2) = P(\text{half of the attribute values are "0" and the other half are "1"}) = \binom{d}{d/2} / 2^d$

...

$P(R= d-2) = P(\text{two attribute values are "0" and all the others are "1"}) = \binom{d}{2} / 2^d$

40

$P(R= d-1) = P(\text{one attribute value is "0" and all the others are "1"}) = \dbinom{d}{1}/2^d$

$P(R=d) = P(\text{all the attribute values are "1"}) = 1/2^d$

These probabilities are drawn from a Binomial distribution with d trials and a probability of success ½. Any binomial distribution can be approximated by a normal distribution, especially if d is large [72].

Theorem 2

The mean and the variance of the Euclidean distances from the origin depend only on the number of dimensions d.

Proof:

We have shown that R Binomial distribution with d trials and a probability of success ½ in each attempt.

In general, if X is Binomially distributed with n tries and probability of success p in each attempt, then $E(X)=pn$ and $V(X)=np(1-p)$. Therefore, in our case:

$\bar{x} = E(R)= dn = 0.5d$

And

$V(R) = d*0.5*0.5 = 0.25d$

Which proofs that both the mean value and the STD depend only on d.

Examples

Below we discuss several numerical examples to better understand the implications of the theorems described above.

In the case of 10 binary dimensions the distribution of the Euclidean distances is given by:

Distance	possible values	Total values	P
R=0	1	1024	0.000976563
R=1	10	1024	0.009765625
R=2	45	1024	0.043945313
R=3	120	1024	0.1171875
R=4	210	1024	0.205078125
R=5	252	1024	0.24609375
R=6	210	1024	0.205078125
R=7	120	1024	0.1171875
R=8	45	1024	0.043945313
R=9	10	1024	0.009765625
R=10	1	1024	0.000976563

Table 1 : Disance distribution for 10 binary variables

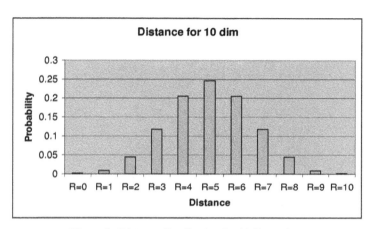

Figure 2 : Distance distribution for 10 dimensions

Variance   2.5
MEAN   5

By Table 1 and Figure 3, the probability of R=0 (all entries in the data point are 'zero') R=1 (only one entry is 'one'), R=10 (all entries are 'one') and R=9 (9 entries are 'one') is very slim. This means that, effectively, most of the data points in this data space lie in the range of R=2 (two entries are 'one' and eight are 'zero') to R=8 (eight entries are 'one', two are 'zero'). So if we limit ourselves to this range, we can reduce the size of the hypercube to accommodate the data space from the original 2^{10} to 2^6. This may not be much. However, this data space is not large anyway.

But consider the case of 100 binary predictors, a similar analysis to the above yields the following distribution of the distances of the data points to the origin:

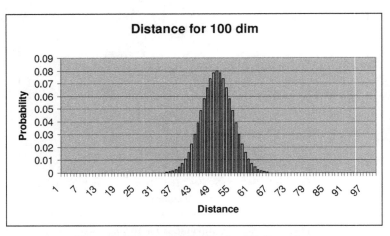

Figure 3 : Distance distribution for 100 dimensions

Variance	25
MEAN	50

By Figure 4, most data points in this data space consists entries with value of 'one' in the range of 37-67. Hence the effective radius of the hypercube to accommodate this dataset is 30, reducing the dimension of the hypercube from the original 2^{100} to 2^{30}, indeed quite a significant reduction.

And, finally, for 500 binary attributes, one can reduce the dimension of hypercube to accommodate the dataset from 2^{500} to approximately 2^{100}.

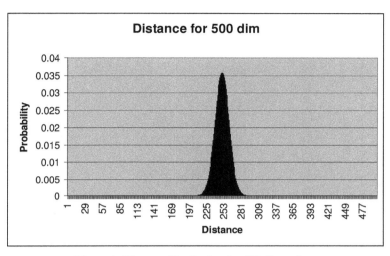

Figure 4 : Distance distribution for 500 dimensions

Variance   125
MEAN   250

In all three cases, the distribution of the distances from the origin is normally distributed with mean and variance values summarized in the table below.

# of Dimensions	Mean	Variance
10	5	2.5
100	50	25
500	250	125

Table 2 : Summary table for different number of binary dimensions

These results are fully compatible with the theorems described above.

Figure 6 tracks the behavior of the STD of the Euclidean distances from the origin for different number of dimension:

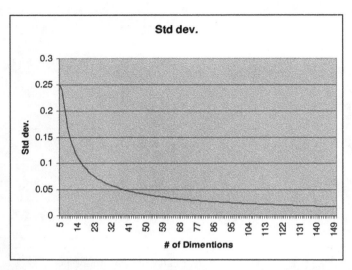

Figure 5 : The relation between the STD and the number of dimensions

This graph shows the behavior pattern of the STD as a function of the number of dimension. Clearly, this pattern agrees with the theorem described above.

3.2.2.2 Continuous Variables

We now extend the analysis above to the case of continuous variables and show that even in this case, the distances of the data points from the origin (the radius) are also normally distributed with STD that decreases as the number of dimensions increases. By distance, in the continuous case, we mean the Euclidean distance. This analysis was done by means of a simulation under various scenarios. We again use several examples to demonstrate this fact. For each case we created random data from the corresponding distribution and calculated the distribution of the distances empirically.

Sample 1

46

In the first case, we created a dataset with 10,000 observations with 3 continuous attributes, each is uniformly distributed in the range of (0,1). For each observation, the distance to the origin was calculated and then the distance distribution was analyzed. For simplicity, we assumed that the three attributes are independent. The results are displayed in Figure 7:

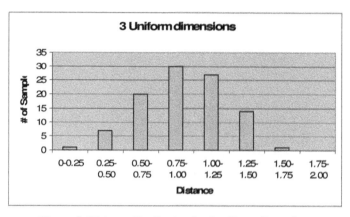

Figure 6 : Distance distribution for 3 uniform dimensions

The next simulation repeated the same scenario but with 10 continuously independent dimensions (same dataset size and same distribution and same parameters). The distance distribution in this case is exhibited in figure 8:

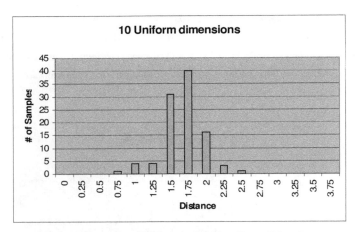

Figure 7 : Distance distribution for 10 uniform dimensions

Finally, we extended the analysis above to the case of 100 continuously and independent uniformly distributed dimensions. The distance distribution is given in Figure 9:

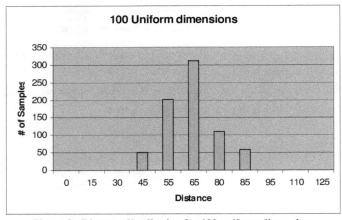

Figure 8 : Distance distribution for 100 uniform dimensions

These three cases show that even when the variables involved are uniformly distributed, the Euclidean distances are also normally distributed. In addition, the effective radius range that covers the distances from the origin of most of the data points is far less than the maximum radius. As with the case of binary variables, the STD of the distribution of the distances also decreases as the number of dimension increases.

Sample 2

We now test the behavior of the distances to the origin for normally-distributed independent variables each in the range (0,1). In each of the cases below, we created randomly 10,000 observations but changed the number of the dimensions involved.

We began with 3 standard normal dimensions, yielding the distance distribution exhibited in Figure 10:

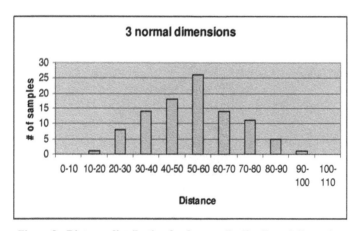

Figure 9 : Distance distribution for 3 normally distributed dimension

Figure 11 presents the corresponding results for 10 standard normally distributed dimensions and Figure 12 for 100 standard normally distributed dimensions.

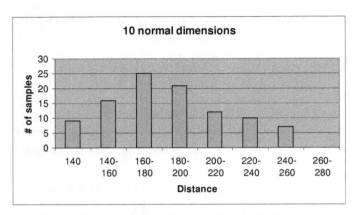

Figure 10 : Distance distribution for 10 normal dimensions

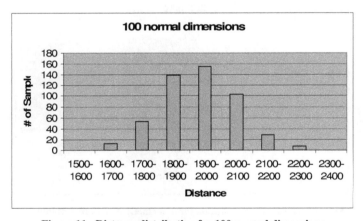

Figure 11 : Distance distribution for 100 normal dimensions

The observations here are similar to those of the uniform distributions, namely that the distribution of the distances of the observations from the origin is approximately normal with the standard deviation of the distribution decreasing as the number of dimensions

50

increases. Again, the effective radius that accommodates the distances from the origin of most data points is substantially smaller than the maximum distance possible.

Sample 3

Finally we consider mixed cases involving binary attributes, uniformly distributed attributes and normally distributed attributes, again drawing 10,000 random observations in each case and analyzing the distribution of the data points from the origin. All attributes are assumed to be independent.

In the first case, we consider 3 dimensions: one uniformly distributed in the range (1,0), one binary variable and one standard normally distributed. The resulting distribution of the Euclidean distances is given in Figure 13:

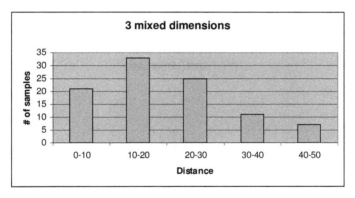

Figure 12 : Distance distribution for 3 mixed dimensions

In the second case, we increased the number of dimensions from 3 to 10: 3 uniformly distributed in the range (0,1), 4 binary variables and 3 standard normally distributed attributes. The result of this simulation is presented in Figure 14.

51

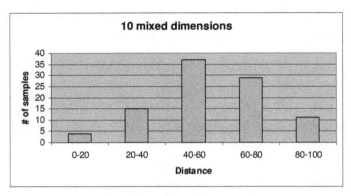

Figure 13 : Distance distribution for 10 mixed dimensions

Finally, we considered the case 100 dimensions of which 30 are uniformly distributed in the range of (0,1), 40 are binary variables and 30 are standard normal variables. Figure 15 exhibits the results of this simulation:

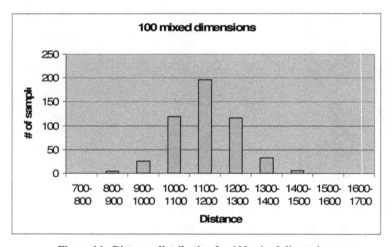

Figure 14 : Distance distribution for 100 mixed dimensions

The conclusions are essentially as above, namely that even in the case of mixed variables, the distances of the data points to the origin is normally distributed and the standard deviation of the normal distribution decreases with the number of dimensions. In addition, a much smaller radius is required to accommodate the radii of most data points.

The practical implication of the above analysis is that in all cases one can significantly reduce the effective size of the space needed to accommodate the data set, regardless of the distribution of the attributes involved. The exact number of dimensions depends on the number of bins for each attribute. But whatever the number of bins, lower dimensional problem spaces will render lower number of cubes for accommodating the data.

3.2.2.3 Discrete Variables

Finally, we expect the same situation to occur also for the case of discrete variables. But because the analysis is basically the same, we will forgo the details.

4 The Cube-Based Approach for Incremental Data Mining

4.1 Introduction

As discussed above, the analytical incremental approach may be limited to relatively simple algorithms and is not general enough to accommodate all data mining problems. To overcome these difficulties, we offer in this work a *cube-based* approach for updating knowledge that works on the data, rather than on the model, which is generic enough to be used by ALL data mining models and algorithms. Instead of storing the model's internal parameters, we use a meta-data approach for representing the data, by summarizing the data in a format which is fairly aggregated, yet detailed enough to ensure that we are not sacrificing a great deal of accuracy. In a manner of speaking, the meta-data in the cube-based approach for updating knowledge is the equivalent to the internal parameters in the analytical approach for knowledge update. Not only does this approach significantly reduce the amount of storage requires to store the data, but, as further described below, the storage space required to store the data is fixed, regardless of the size of the database. This means that even as new observations arrive, the size of the cube-based dataset does not change.

We take advantage of this property and use the cube-based data representation to update knowledge instead of using the original dataset itself. As a result, we are not concerned about new data increasing the size of the database indefinitely because the size of cube-based datasets is fixed. This then allows one to re-run the data mining procedure anew for each batch of new observations by applying the non-incremental data mining model on the entire set of data. As a result there is no loss in information because we do not discard any observations from the modeling process, nor do we run into the problem discussed above that the analytical approach may not always be extended to work incrementally. Later on we show that not only that the cube-based approach results in significant savings in storage requirements, but also that the accuracy level of the updated knowledge is comparable to that of the non-incremental approach.

54

In this section we describe the cube-based approach for representing data. We start by describing the need for the cube model, we then lay the foundation for the cube-based approach, followed by several examples on the use of the cubes. We then continue with the description of the benefits of using the cube-based approach for incremental data mining.

4.2 The Cube Model

4.2.1 Multi-Dimensional Histograms

The cube-based approach is based on multidimensional histograms [31] which is a way to save summary information for multi-dimensional data. While this approach has many applications for data management, it has not used thus far in the context of data mining and updating knowledge.

The basic concept of multi-dimensional histograms is to divide the space of possible values (the problem space) into buckets, saving only the information which corresponds to these buckets rather than the entire dataset itself. Essentially, multi dimensional histograms offer a different way of representing the data that result in a significant savings in the storage requirements for the data. The accuracy level of the new data representation depends on the resolution level used to define those "buckets". Indeed, there is a tradeoff between accuracy and storage space. Higher accuracy requires higher data resolution (i.e., more "buckets") and thus more meta-data elements to store and vice versa.

Additional information on multi-dimensional histograms and their uses can be found in the literature review chapter above.

One can easily note the similarity between multi-dimensional histograms and the OLAP in data warehouses, as both use cubes to summarize and store data.
The main difference between these two approaches is that in the cube-based approach,

the cubes represent but a small fraction of the problem space, with each containing the number of data points that "belong" to the cube, while in the OLAP approach the cubes summarize data at different classifications (none of which are related to their location on the problem's space).

4.2.2 The Cube Approach for Data Representation

In the original problem space, each observation is represented by a point (vector) in a multi-dimensional space, where the number of dimensions (coordinates) is equal to the number of attributes (predictors, dimensions). In data mining applications, the number of observations is very large, in the order of magnitude of millions or more, and the number of attributes is in the order of magnitude of hundreds or more. This renders an excessively large data space. Clearly, this space can not be stored in memory. The cube-based approach solves this problem by saving the (approximate) location of each data point (observation) using a fixed amount of storage regardless of how big the dataset is.

For example, let us examine the case of a two dimensional problem, with two continuous variables X and Y, each categorized into 10 bins. The data can be represented by a 10x10 two-dimensional histogram with 100 cells, as described in Figure 16. One can collapse the X and Y variable into fewer "bins" thereby manage with a smaller 2-dimensional histogram to represent the data.

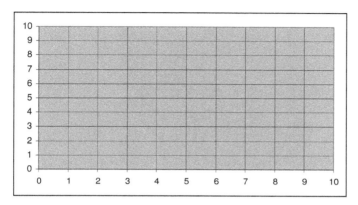

Figure 15 : Two dimensional histograms

In case the data points consists of 3 dimensions (attributes) with three values each, the multi-dimensional histogram is defined by a 3x3x3 cube, as described in Figure 17.

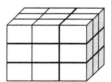

Figure 16 : Three dimensional histogram

The diagram above describes the split of the problem's space into multi-dimensional cubes. As we will show below, in high dimensional space not all the cubes are populated, and as a result need not be stored. Figure 18 portrays this case graphically for the three dimensional cube above, but containing only the cells that are populated. So instead of the original 27 cubes, only 13 cubes are required to store the data in this case.

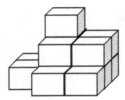

Figure 17 : Three dimensional histogram with truncated cubes

The same logic which was described above for 2 and 3 dimensional problem's space can be applied to higher multi-dimensional spaces.

Now, instead of saving the original data points, in the cube approach we save only the cube location and number of data points which are contained in each cube.

For example, imagine a two dimensional space with two continuous variables, in the range of 1-100 each, which are binned into 10 equally-sized categories: 0-10, 11-20, 21-30,…, as described in Figure 16. Given an observation vector, say (9, 73), this vector belongs to the cube (1,7), or the 61st cell, in the two-dimensional histogram above. So instead of storing the vector (1,7) for this observation, in the cube approach we only store the cube location 61 and the number of data points in the dataset that fall into this cell.

Assuming that we have a 2 dimensional dataset, each dimension in the range of 1-256 (just to make things simpler), then in order to store a dataset of 100,000 observations we will require:

100,000 (observations) * 2 (dimensions) * 8 (bits per attribute value) = 1,600,000 bits

Storing the same dataset in the cube approach requires, in the worst case scenario, 100 cubes (= 10^2) to represent the entire data space and a storage space of:

100 (number of cubes) * 8 (bits to store the cube number) * 8 (bits to store the number of samples in each cube) = 6,400 bits

Indeed, quite a reduction in storage requirements.

As we will show below, in real life cases only a small percentage of the cubes are actually populated and most of them will be empty. Since we only store the non-empty cells, the reduction in storage requirements will even be greater. For example, if only 25% of the cubes are populated, the actual storage requirement is:

25 (number of populated cubes) * 8 (bits to store the cube number) * 8 (bits to store the number of samples in each cube) = 1,600 bits

This represents 0.1% of the amount of storage required for the full dataset! Furthermore, the savings in storage requirements increases as the number of dimensions increases. For example, in a 100 dimensional space, one needs to store 100 numbers to represent each observation (data point), versus only two numbers in the cube approach – one for storing the location of the data point, and the other to store the number of data points falling in this cube.

Not only is the storage space required in the cube approach far less than the amount of storage required to store the data in the original form, but the storage space in the cube-based approach is fixed, depending only on the number of cubes, regardless of the number of observations! The amount of storage does not change even when new observations arrive, because all one needs to do is to update the counter of the corresponding cube (and their classification) to which the new data belongs to. Thus the amount of storage required to save the data does not change.

4.2.3 Estimating an Upper Bound of the Number of Cubes to Represent the Data

For binary and categorical predictors we have a way to calculate at the outset an upper bound on the number of cubes required to accommodate the dataset. In order to accomplish this we offer a different way of storing the dataset. Instead of storing the original data point itself, we store the locations of the '1' values in the data point. For example, the observation, with 15 binary dimensions, (0,1,0,0,0,1,0,0,0,0,1,0,0,0,0) will be represented by the vector (2,6,11), where the values '2', '6' and '11' correspond to the locations, respectively, of the '1' values of the original data point.

Clearly, no information whatsoever is lost by representing the data point using the "location" vector. This representation allows one to store the data point with fewer dimensions (e.g., 3 instead of 15, in the above example). But more importantly, recall that in the binary case the radius of each data point is given by the number of entries with the value of '1', which, by definition, is also the length of the location vector. For instance, the data vector above contains three 1's which is also the radius of this point and the dimension (length) of the location vector. Since, as shown above, the distribution of the length of the location vector is normal with known parameters, we can calculate a 95% confidence interval for the dimension of the location vectors. Let R denotes the size of the confidence interval (given, approximately, by twice the standard deviation of the radiuses of the data points in the dataset).

We use this confidence interval to estimate an upper bound on the number of cubes to accommodate the data. Recall that moving from the original data representation to the location representation changes the dimensions of each entry from binary to ordinal, and assuming that each of these ordinal dimensions is expressed by means of d bins (d is the dimension of the original data vector), the number of cubes required to accommodate the data, in the worst case, is R^d.

Now, for the original data representation, the maximum number of cubes to accommodate the data is 2^d. But because, as demonstrated above, the size of R is much smaller than d, the number of cubes required to store the data using the location vector format is much lower. In practice, however, the number of the required cubes will be even much smaller than this because of the property that we discussed above that multi-dimensional data is sparsely populated. Furthermore, this analysis corresponds to the worst case scenario, and usually practical applications tend to "behave" more elegantly than in the worst case. In the next section we describe an approximation method to estimate the actual number of cubes to represent a given set of data.

4.2.4 Approximating the Actual Number of Cubes to Represent the Data

We offer an approximate algorithm to estimate the number of cubes needed to represent the data.

The basis for the approximation model is the linear relationship which exists between the number of observations and the number of cubes. Based on this understanding the following algorithm has been created:

- Determine the bin size for each of the non-binary dimensions of the problem. These bin sizes will determine the size of the cubes.
- Take a representative sample of observations from the entire dataset, which is large enough to give a complete picture of the data distribution, yet not too large to hamper the calculation process. A good rule of thumb is to take a sample consisting of 10-20% of the data observations.
- Run cube approach on the chosen sample and ascertain the required number of cubes to accommodate the sample data.
- Calculate the 'cube ratio' n/m, where n denotes the number of data observations and m the actual number of cubes required to represent this data.
- Extrapolate the required number of cubes needed for the entire dataset applying the cube ratio above to the number of observations in the entire dataset.

For example, when we loaded 10,000 samples from the "real life" database used in this work (see chapter 6 for details), 6,817 cubes were needed. Based on that we can extrapolate that for 50,000 samples we will need 34,085 cubes. When we loaded the actual 50,000 DMEF samples into cube 37,980 cubes were needed. Therefore, with a

61

very simple calculation we got a pretty good estimate for the number of cubes (10% error).

4.3 Reducing Noise with the Cube-Based Approach

The previous section has shown that in most real life dataset we can reduce the number of dimensions to represent the data by means of the cube approach. In addition to reducing storage, the cube model is also capable of "reducing" the noise in the dataset, which affects the quality of the model. This section will describe the theoretical model of noise reduction using cubes.

4.3.1 Noisy Data

Modern databases are often plagued by noisy data [73]. Reasons for noisy data include, among many others, measurement errors, typing errors, and combining data from different sources. Processing noisy data often results in less accurate and biased models. To prevent such situations, data is usually pre-processed and cleaned before modeling. But even with preprocessing, there is no guarantee that one can eliminate all of the noise in the data. This gives an advantage to data mining algorithms which possess an inherent capability to filter noise. We show below that the cube-based approach for data representation has this capability by "absorbing" some of the error in the data. This is particularly true for noise which results from measurement errors.

The idea is very simple.

Let $(x_1, x_2, ..., x_d)$ denote the "clean" data point. Then consider the same point with noise $(x_1 + \alpha_1, x_2 + \alpha_2, ..., x_d + \alpha_d)$, where the $\alpha_j's$ are the noise terms.

Now in the cube-based representation, we expect that x_i and $x_i + \alpha_i$ reside in the same cubes for most, if not all, of the dimensions. This has the effect of truncating the error terms, allowing one to build the model based for the most part on "clean" data points. The result is a more accurate model. We note, however, that the noise reduction applies primarily to continuous variables, because these variables are more susceptible to measurement errors than binary predictors.

4.3.2 A Simulated Example

We use a simulated example to demonstrate the property above. We begin by creating a "noiseless" dataset that contains 2,500 samples each with 10 independent and uniformly distributed attributes in the range of (0,10). Next, we add uniformly-distributed noise to this dataset to create several datasets, each with a different noise level. The results are described in the table 3:

Noise Level	Cube Size	Cumm. Data err	Cumm. Cube err
1	1	2804.67	1988.055
0.75	1	2103.859	1851.675
0.7	1	1970.427	1863.356
0.6	1	1687.701	1900.634
0.5	1	1409.396	1987.421
0.25	1	703.5723	2323.814
2	2	5621.5	3976.471
1.8	2	5041.709	3801.693
1.5	2	4227.009	3712.022
1.4	2	3940.659	3723.851
1.3	2	3649.299	3745.625
1.2	2	3382.231	3821.504
1	2	2813.386	3961.611

Table 3 : Noise reduction for uniformly distributed noise

- *Noise level* – the maximum noise level (the upper bound of the uniform distribution).
- *Cube size* – the size of the cube used
- *Cumm Data err* – the sum of differences between the noisy data and the noiseless data calculated by:

$$\text{Cumulative data error} = \sum_{i=1}^{n} \sqrt{\sum_{j=1}^{d} \left(x_{i,j} - \overline{x_{i,j}}\right)^2}$$

Where $x_{i,j}$ denotes the jth dimension in the ith dimension of the original observation and $\overline{x_{i,j}}$ denotes the jth dimension in the ith dimension of the noisy sample.

- *Cumm Cube err* – the sum of differences between the center of the cube and the noiseless data points, given by:

$$\text{Cumulative cube error} = \sum_{i=1}^{n}\sqrt{\sum_{j=1}^{d}\left(\hat{x}_{i,j} - \overline{x_{i,j}}\right)^2}$$

Where $\hat{x}_{i,j}$ denotes the jth dimension in the ith dimension of the cubes that contains this data sample, And $\overline{x_{i,j}}$ denotes the jth dimension in the ith dimension of the noisy sample.

The table above indicates that for noise level 1 and cube size of 1, the sum of distances over all the dimensions between the original data and the noisy data was 2804.67, whereas the sum of differences over all the dimensions between the cube data and the noisy data was only 1988.055. This implies that using the cube-based data has created a dataset which is more similar to the original dataset.

Furthermore, we can see from the table that for cube size of 1 and noise level less than 0.7, the cube-based data is more similar to the original data than the actual "noisy" data. For cube size of 2, the cube-based data is more similar to the original data than the actual "noisy" data if the noise level was less then 1.4.

This result can also be used to ascertain the cube size required to handle noisy data. By the above analysis, the cube size should be larger than the ratio *excepted noise / 0.7*. For example, for a variable in the range of 0-10 and noise level which is uniformly distributed over the range [0, 2], the cube size should be larger then 2 / 0.7 = 2.85.

We have also extended this experiment to the case where the error levels are distributed according to the standard normal distribution. The results for this case are presented in

Table 4:

Noise Average	Noise STD	Cube Size	Cumm. Data err	Cumm. Cube err
0	1.45	1	5068.553	4994.22
0	1.25	1	4394.906	4371.886
0	1	1	3718.813	3738.267
0	0.87	1	3051.782	3133.442

Table 4 : Noise reduction for normally distributed noise

In this case, when the STD of the noise is larger than 1, using the cubes give better results than using the actual noisy data. This is because the cubes absorb some of the noise in the data. As demonstrated above, this result can also be used to predict the cube size required to handle normally distributed noisy data.

The problem is that in real life situations, the level of noise is not known in advance, making it impossible to predict the cube size to accommodate noise. There is a tradeoff here. Using larger cubes allows absorbing more noise but may produce less accurate knowledge. Using smaller cubes purportedly results in a more accurate model but this model can be hampered by noise.

One possible way to handle this tradeoff between noise and accuracy is by processing the data with different cubes sizes and seeking the cube size which yields the best performance on a validation dataset. This is one aspect of the cubes size calibration process which is further discussed later in this work.

4.4 Knowledge Update Using the Cubes

With the cube-based approach to represent data, we can describe the knowledge update procedure in Figure 19 as a three-layered diagram:

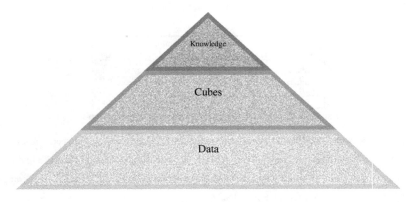

Figure 18 : Data pyramid

- Data - the lowest layer containing the original data points to be processed.
- Cubes – the "meta-data" representation of the original data points
- Knowledge – updating knowledge is based on the cubes

The cube-based approach for updating knowledge proceeds as follows:

1. Initialization step
    a. Categorize all the non binary variables in the dataset
    b. Define the boundaries of the problem space
    c. Determine how many cubes are required to represent the data
    d. Divide the data space into multi-dimensional histograms (cubes), as follows:
       - Each cube represents part of the problem space.
       - Each cube has a specific location.
       - The set of cubes cover the entire problem space.
       - The number of cubes is pre-defined and fixed.

2. Update the meta-data for new observations:

66

a. Read a new data point

b. Find the cube to which this data point belongs

c. Increase the number of data points in this cube by 1 to update the cube

3. Update the knowledge

a. Apply the non incremental algorithm on the cube data to rebuild the model and update knowledge

4. For each new data point, return to step 2.

Practically, this approach is usually conducted in a batch mode, updating the cubes and modifying knowledge each period (every week, for example) or after obtaining a larget enough set of new observations.

Note that this approach for knowledge update is independent neither of the way the cubes are defined and updated (step #2), nor on the algorithm for updating knowledge (step #3), thus making it a generic approach to deal with knowledge update for a variety of problems and different knowledge formats. In the sequel to this dissertation we will implement this approach to a variety of data mining algorithms and comparing the quality of the models obtained using this approach to the traditional non incremental algorithms to update knowledge based on the original entire dataset.

4.5 Data Representation in the Cube Based Approach

We now describe the cube-based approach for knowledge update in greater detail.

Let X denote the original data matrix with elements $x_{i,j}$:

$$X = \begin{pmatrix} x_{1,1} & \cdots & x_{1,d} \\ \cdots & & \cdots \\ x_{n,1} & \cdots & x_{n,d} \end{pmatrix}$$

Where:

d is the number of data dimensions

n is the number of observations.

For the simplicity of the discussion but without effecting its generality, we will assume that dimensions 1 to k (where $k < d$) are continuous, and dimensions $k+1$ to *d* are binary.

The first step is to express the original data in the cube format, represented by the matrix Z:

$$Z = \begin{pmatrix} c_1 & c_2 & \ldots & c_p \\ b_1 & b_2 & \ldots & b_p \\ m_1 & m_2 & \ldots & m_p \end{pmatrix}$$

Where:

c_i is the cube number for the continuous variables $(x_{i,1}, \ldots, x_{i,k})$

b_i is the cube number for the binary variables $(x_{i,k+1}, \ldots, x_{i,d})$

m_i is the number of data vectors containing both c_i and b_i

p is the number of cubes

The Z described above is the generic case, when all the data variables are binary then the first row of the Z matrix can be eliminated, thus creating a Z matrix that will be:

$$BinaryOnlyZ = \begin{pmatrix} b_1 & b_2 & \ldots & b_p \\ m_1 & m_2 & \ldots & m_p \end{pmatrix}$$

Where:

b_i is the cube number for the binary variables $(x_{i,k+1}, \ldots, x_{i,n})$

m_i is the number of data vectors containing both c_i and b_i

n is the number of cubes

The algorithm to convert the X matrix to the Z matrix is quite simple, and based on the following assumptions:

- All continuous dimensions are split into a fixed number or bins, e.g. there is the same number of bins for each one of the continuous dimensions.
- Each of the binary variables is split into 2 bins.
- Each data sample contain of continuous variables ($x_{i,1}$, ... , $x_{i,k}$) and binary variables ($x_{i,k+1}$, ... , $x_{i,n}$)

These assumptions were only created to make the conversion algorithm easier to understand.

The algorithm is:

- Set p = 0
- For each observation i,
    a. For each continues dimension j ($j=1...k$), find the bin number to which $x_{i,j}$ belongs.

    $$b_{i,j} = \left\lfloor \frac{x_{i,j}}{r} \right\rfloor$$

    Where,

    $x_{i,j}$ is the value of the jth dimension in the ith observation

    $B_{i,j}$ is the bin number to which $x_{i,j}$ belongs to

    r is the number of bins on the continues dimensions (see assumption #1 above)

    b. Combine the $b_{i,j}$ (where $j=1..,k$) values to find the cube to which the ith observation belongs to, using the following equation:

    $$continuous\_cube\_number = \sum_{j=0}^{k} b_{i,j} * r^{j}$$

    Where,

    $b_{i,j}$ is the bin number to which $x_{i,j}$ belongs

    r is the number of bins on the continues dimensions

    j is the dimension

    c. For each binary dimension j ($j=k+1,...,d$), find the bin number to which $x_{i,j}$ belongs.

69

$$b_{i,j} = \begin{cases} 0 & x_{i,j} = 0 \\ 1 & x_{i,j} = 1 \end{cases}$$

Where,

$x_{i,j}$ is the value of the jth dimension in the ith observation

$B_{i,j}$ is the bin number to which $x_{i,j}$ belongs to

d. Combine the $b_{i,j}$ *(where j=k+1..,d)* values to find the cube to which the ith observation belongs to, using the following equation:

$$binary\_cube\_number = \sum_{j=0}^{k} b_{i,j} * 2^{j}$$

Where,

$b_{i,j}$ is the bin number to which $x_{i,j}$ belongs

r is the number of bins on the continues dimensions

j is the dimension

e. Check the Z matrix to see if it already contains a column with the *continuous _cube_number* and the *binary_cube_number* calculcated above. If so, increment the counter (*m*) for this column.

If not, add a new column to the Z matrix $\begin{pmatrix} continuous\_cube\_number \\ binary\_cube\_number \\ 1 \end{pmatrix}$

and increment the value of p.

We use a simple example to demonstrate this transformation process from the X matrix to the Z matrix. Assuming the problem's space has 10 observations, each with 5 continuous dimensions in the range of 0-10 and 3 binary variables, as follows:

Obs. 1: 5.38, 8.89, 0.09, 1.53, 1.82, 1, 1, 0;

Obs. 2: 6.61, 8.69, 4.84, 0.67, 4.91, 0, 1, 0;

Obs. 3: 7.77, 7.04, 0.40, 7.02, 6.96, 1, 1, 1;

Obs. 4: 2.70, 7.50, 2.92, 8.42. 6.63, 1, 0, 1;

Obs. 5: 9.19, 3.29, 0.82, 1.77, 6.32, 0, 1, 0;

Obs. 6: 4.52, 3.80, 7.06, 3.39, 2.99, 1, 0, 0;

Obs. 7: 3.69, 7.72, 6.99, 0.59, 5.83, 0, 1, 1;

Obs. 8: 6.53, 6.62, 9.93, 1.74, 8.49, 0, 1, 1;

Obs. 9: 3.40, 1.53, 7.24, 4.45, 0.26, 1, 0, 1;

Obs. 10: 5.07, 9.50, 1.71, 1.61, 0.48, 1, 1, 0;

The X matrix is given by:

$$X = \begin{pmatrix} 5.38 & 8.89 & 0.09 & 1.53 & 1.82 & 1 & 1 & 0 \\ 6.61 & 8.69 & 4.84 & 0.67 & 4.91 & 0 & 1 & 0 \\ 7.77 & 7.04 & 0.40 & 7.02 & 6.96 & 1 & 1 & 1 \\ 2.70 & 7.50 & 2.92 & 8.42 & 6.63 & 1 & 0 & 1 \\ 9.19 & 3.29 & 0.82 & 1.77 & 6.32 & 0 & 1 & 0 \\ 4.52 & 3.80 & 7.06 & 3.39 & 2.99 & 1 & 0 & 0 \\ 3.69 & 7.72 & 6.99 & 0.59 & 5.83 & 0 & 1 & 1 \\ 6.53 & 6.62 & 9.93 & 1.74 & 8.49 & 0 & 1 & 1 \\ 3.40 & 1.53 & 7.24 & 4.45 & 0.26 & 1 & 0 & 1 \\ 5.07 & 9.50 & 1.71 & 1.61 & 0.48 & 1 & 1 & 0 \end{pmatrix}$$

Now, as a first example, we split each continuous dimension into 10 equally-sized bins each of length 1, such that the first bin represents data values between 0-1, the second bin data values 1-2, etc. The binary dimensions have been split into 2 bins, 0's and 1's.

Following the algorithm described above, the resulting Z matrix for this dataset is:

$$Z = \begin{pmatrix} 58011 & 68404 & 77076 & 27286 & 93016 & 43732 & 37605 & 66918 & 31740 & 59110 \\ 6 & 2 & 7 & 5 & 2 & 4 & 3 & 3 & 5 & 6 \\ 1 & 1 & 1 & 1 & 1 & 1 & 1 & 1 & 1 & 1 \end{pmatrix}$$

For example, looking on the first observation, (5.38, 8.89, 0.09, 1.53, 1.82, 1, 1, 0). The continuous variables for this observation vector occupies the 5th bin on the first dimension, the 8th bin on the second dimension, the 0th bin on third dimension, the 1st bin on the fourth dimension and the 1st bin on the fifth dimension. For the binary variables it occupies the 1st bin on the first dimension, the 1st bin on the second dimension and the 0th

bin on the third dimension.

Given the formulas described above, the *continuous_cube_value* and the *binary_cube_value* for this observation will be:

$continuous\_cube\_value = 5*10^4+8*10^3+0*10^2+1*10^1+1*10^0=58011$

$binary\_cube\_value = 1*2^2+1*2^1+0*2^0=6$

Therefore, the first column in the Z matrix is $\begin{pmatrix} 58011 \\ 6 \\ 1 \end{pmatrix}$

The same logic can be applied to all other observations thus creating the Z matrix described above. Note that only 10 pairs of cubes are required to represent the data in this case.

Also note that in this simple example each pair of cube contained only one data point. As a result all the values in the third row of matrix Z are equal to 1. In real life this is rarely the case, and usually one cube contains several data points.

The Z matrix is not amenable to data mining. So in the second stage of the transformation process we convert the Z matrix into another matrix, which we denote by W, which is in the form of the original data matrix X:

$$W = \begin{pmatrix} w_{1,1} & \cdots & w_{d,1} \\ \cdots & & \cdots \\ w_{n,d} & \cdots & w_{n,d} \end{pmatrix}$$

Where $w_{i,j}$ is the location of the ith dimension of the x_j data cube.

The conversion of the Z matrix into the W matrix is done using the following algorithm:

For each column $z_i = \begin{pmatrix} c_i \\ b_i \\ m_i \end{pmatrix}$ in the Z matrix,

Perform the following steps m_i times

- Convert c_i into its location in the problem space
- Convert b_i into its location in the problem space
- Add a row to the existing W matrix that contain the converted c_i and b_i

In the example above, the W matrix is:

$$W = \begin{pmatrix} 5 & 8 & 0 & 1 & 1 & 1 & 1 & 0 \\ 6 & 8 & 4 & 0 & 4 & 0 & 1 & 0 \\ 7 & 7 & 0 & 7 & 6 & 1 & 1 & 1 \\ 2 & 7 & 2 & 8 & 6 & 1 & 0 & 1 \\ 9 & 3 & 0 & 1 & 6 & 0 & 1 & 0 \\ 4 & 3 & 7 & 3 & 2 & 1 & 0 & 0 \\ 3 & 7 & 6 & 0 & 5 & 0 & 1 & 1 \\ 6 & 6 & 9 & 1 & 8 & 0 & 1 & 1 \\ 3 & 1 & 7 & 4 & 0 & 1 & 0 & 1 \\ 5 & 9 & 1 & 1 & 0 & 1 & 1 & 0 \end{pmatrix}$$

For example, let's examine how we create the W vector for the first observation. The Z vector for the first row is $\begin{pmatrix} 58011 \\ 6 \\ 1 \end{pmatrix}$. Following the procedure above, c_i, whose value is

58011, corresponds to the 5th bin the first dimension, 8th bin on the second dimension, 0th bin on the third dimension, 1st bin on the forth dimension and 1st bin on the fifth dimension. In addition, b_i whose value is 6, corresponds to the 1st bin on the first binary dimension, 1st bin on the second binary dimension and 0th bin on the third binary dimension. Combining the results for c_i and b_i we get (5, 8, 0, 1, 1, 1, 1, 0) which is the first row of the W matrix described above.

As another example, we consider the case of a cruder cube resolution. Instead of 10 bins for each continuous dimension, as above, we now consider 5 bins for each continuous dimension, denoted as bin #0, …,bin#4, each of size 2, representing the data values 0-2, 2-4, 4-6, 6-8, and 8-10, respectively. For the binary variables we still use 2 bins for each dimension.

Now, taking the first observation, as an example,
(5.38, 8.89, 0.09, 1.53, 1.82, 1, 1, 0), For the continuous variables, it belongs to bin number 2, 4, 0, 0, 0 in the 5-dimensional cube, respectively. The cube location is given by: $2*5^4+4*5^3+0*5^2+0*5^1+0*5^0 = 1750$
For the binary variables, it belongs to bin number 1, 1, 0 which is translated into $1*2^2+1*2^1+0*2^0=6$ (same as above).

Note that this cube location also applies to the last observation (5.07, 9.50, 1.71, 1.61, 0.48, 1, 1, 0). As a result, the value of m_i in the first column of the Z matrix will be 2.

The corresponding Z matrix and W matrix for this example are:

$$Z = \begin{pmatrix} 1750 & 3052 & 2268 & 1048 & 2628 & 1456 & 1077 & 2354 & 710 \\ 6 & 2 & 7 & 5 & 2 & 4 & 3 & 3 & 5 \\ 2 & 1 & 1 & 1 & 1 & 1 & 1 & 1 & 1 \end{pmatrix}$$

$$W = \begin{pmatrix} 4 & 8 & 0 & 0 & 0 & 1 & 1 & 0 \\ 4 & 8 & 0 & 0 & 0 & 1 & 1 & 0 \\ 6 & 8 & 4 & 0 & 4 & 0 & 1 & 0 \\ 6 & 6 & 0 & 6 & 6 & 1 & 1 & 1 \\ 2 & 6 & 2 & 8 & 6 & 1 & 0 & 1 \\ 8 & 2 & 0 & 0 & 6 & 0 & 1 & 0 \\ 4 & 2 & 6 & 2 & 2 & 1 & 0 & 0 \\ 2 & 6 & 6 & 0 & 4 & 0 & 1 & 1 \\ 6 & 6 & 8 & 0 & 8 & 0 & 1 & 1 \\ 2 & 0 & 6 & 4 & 0 & 1 & 0 & 1 \end{pmatrix}$$

It is not surprising that using fewer number of bins (5 instead of 10) results in a W matrix which is less accurate (i.e., less similar to the original data). But the benefit is that it requires a smaller Z matrix, thus saving memory. Indeed, there exists a tradeoff between the accuracy level and storage requirements with more accuracy requiring more storage requirements and vice versa. One needs to strike a balance between accuracy and storage requirements for each problem being considered.

Once the data has been represented in the cube format, one can invoke the non-incremental data mining algorithm on the cube data in order to update knowledge. For example, in the case of linear regression, one applies the least squares method to estimate the model parameters on the cube-based data, using the matrix W instead of the matrix X. The main benefit is that one uses a fixed amount of storage to represent the data, regardless of the number of observations involved.

Furthermore, whenever new data arrives, all that one needs to do is to update the Z matrix to account for the new observation and the W matrix, accordingly. As demonstrated above, both of these operations are quite simple and do not require that one reconsiders the already existing data points.

This section has used an example of continuous variables and binary variables. The same savings in storage space also applies when the variables are ordinal or of every other type. In any case, converting the actual data point to the cube it belongs to dramatically reduces the amount of memory needed in order to store the data.
For example: assuming we have the following observation (1,0,1,1,0) in a 5 binary dimensions problem space, then using the cubes representation this sample will belong to cube number $1*2^4+0*2^3+1*2^2+1*2^1+0*2^0 = 22$. Thus instead of saving the observation (1,0,1,1,0) all we need to do is save the cube to which it belongs (22).

4.5.1 The Benefits of Using the Cube Approach for Incremental Data Mining

The cube approach has been created in order to allow incremental algorithms to save a detailed yet limited amount of information regarding the processed observations, thus allowing it to make the best decision when new observations are processed.

Letting the data mining algorithm use the cubes instead of the original data has many advantages:

- **The cubes matrix is much smaller then the X matrix** -
  Using the Z matrix prevents the need to save the entire data set and thus save a lot of storage space, as described in the previous section.

- **Adding a new sample requires adding less information** -
  When adding a new sample to the X matrix, we add d new values (a row in the X matrix). While, when adding a new value to the Z matrix we are only adding 3 new values (a new column in the Z matrix), and therefore adding a new sample to the cube matrix is much more efficient.

- **Amount of observation is not directly related to the amount of needed storage** – Adding a new observation to the X matrix require adding a new row, while in the Z matrix there are many cases where a new observation falls into one of the cubes which is already described in the matrix and then all that needs to be done is increment the counter for this cube – no data needs to be added to the Z matrix.

- **The cubes accuracy level can be controlled** -
  Larger cube resolution (smaller cubes) results in more accuracy representation in the Z matrix, but the storage requirements increase (less chance for multiple data samples in the same cube). The reverse hold true as well.
  Therefore, one can control the accuracy level of the cube approach by defining the number of cubes, subject to memory constraints.

- **Support different types of data mining algorithms** -
  The cubes contain information which is detailed enough to support different types of data mining algorithms (regression, classification etc.). This feature will be

76

further demonstrated in the next chapters where the cube-based approach is applied on different incremental algorithms.

- **Creating the Z matrix is simple** -
  The algorithm to create the Z matrix described above. It has been shown that it is quite a simple and straight-forward algorithm, no complex calculations are needed to create the Z matrix.

- **Support both parameters update and coefficient update** –
  using the "cube" model the incremental algorithm can perform both parameter update and coefficient updates, thus affording it the flexibility to arrive at the optimum model.

Using the Z matrix in incremental algorithm has many advantages, but it requires modifying the algorithm to use the Z matrix instead of the original observations (X matrix). There are cases where this change is simple, like in the algorithm described in section 8.9 which discusses a Z based K-means incremental algorithm. But in cases where this change is not simple or not possible, the W matrix can be used instead.

The W matrix has the same structure as the X matrix. Thus, one can apply the original, non-incremental, data mining algorithm directly on the W matrix. While this may not render the data mining algorithm more efficient, this is compensated by the substantial reduction in storage volume to contain the data, which is not even dependent on the number of (incremental) observations.

Having said this, we note that while the X matrix usually contains real numbers, the W matrix, by the way it is structured, contains only integer numbers. Now, using only integer numbers allows saving in storage space, since a short integer value can be represented using 2 bytes only whereas a real number is represented using 8 bytes. Hence, the amount of storage space needed to save the W matrix can be as low as 4 times less then the amount of storage needed to save the X matrix. We also note that some algorithms may work faster with integer data than with non integer data. From this perspective, working with the W matrix instead of the X matrix may results in a much more efficient algorithm, as performing mathematical calculation on simple data type (int) is much simpler than performing mathematical calculation on more complicated data types.

Furthermore, the real benefit of the data mining algorithm result if one can store all data in memory, because operations with CPU are much faster than operations involving hard disk. In data mining applications, which are characterized by millions of rows and hundreds of columns, it is usually impossible to store the X matrix in memory, whereas it might be with the W matrix, because it only involves integer values. This in and out of itself render a substantial saving in running the data mining algorithms, and justifies the use of a W-type matrix rather an X-type matrix.

Basically, this all boils down to a tradeoff between storage requirements and quality of the data mining models. We plan to study this tradeoff in the subsequent chapters for the primary class models in data mining.

4.6 Conclusions

In this chapter we described the cube-based approach for data representation which divides the problem space into fixed-sized multi-dimensional cubes. The original dataset is then mapped into these multi-dimensional cubes, saving only the location of each data point in the hypercube. Because multi dimensional data spaces are sparsely populated, this yields substantial savings in the amount of storage to store the dataset.

5 Pre-Processing

5.1 Introduction

Often some pre-processing is required to convert the data to a form which is amenable for data mining. In most cases, preprocessing the data takes the major effort in building a data mining model.

In this dissertation we are interested in preprocessing which affects the multi dimensional cube model. To avoid confusion, we refer to the "conventional" preprocessing methods as non-incremental preprocessing and to the preprocessing required for constructing and modifying the cubes as incremental preprocessing.

5.2 Non-Incremental Pre-Processing

In the non incremental case, preprocessing is conducted on the entire dataset prior to running the data mining model. The objective is to prepare the ground for data mining. A number of different tools and methods are often used for non-incremental pre-processing of data [76]:

- *Sampling*, which selects a representative subset from a large population of data;
- *Transformation*, which manipulates the raw data
- *Denoising*, which removes noise from data;
- *Normalization*, which organizes data for more efficient access; and
- *Feature extraction*, which pulls out specified data that is significant in some particular context.

The pre-processing process often requires scanning the entire dataset to calculate statistical properties of the variables involved and then using these characteristics to preprocess the data. For example, to standardize a variable, one needs to estimate the mean value and the standard deviation of the variable across all observations. Other important aspect of non-incremental preprocessing is data hygiene, cleansing, consolidating records, merge/purge, outlier analysis, and more.

5.3 Incremental Pre-Processing

Even after the original data has been cleansed, incremental pre-processing is needed in order to convert each new data sample into its appropriate cube.
This process can be split into two parts:

- Initial pre-processing – applies to the preprocessing the existing original dataset in order to create the initial cube base data representation
- Incremental pre-processing – applies to preprocessing the incremental data, as it comes along, in order to determine the location (cube) of each new data point. The incremental preprocessing might also affect the structure and the number of the cubes for representing the data.

5.3.1 Initial Pre-Processing

This step analyses each variable in the original dataset in order to decide how to represent it in the cube-based approach. This process is known as discretization as we convert all the variables in discrete values stored into the cubes. There has been quite a lot of work done previously on discretization and [133] gives a review of the different discretization methods and compare their performance. [134] review a set of more advanced discretization methods (used mostly for naive-Bayes learning) and show the benefits of them. Another approach is presented in [135] where the authors present a new method which takes into account the interdependencies between attributes.

In this work we have chosen to take the simple "binning" approach for two main reasons: First, as the binning is very simple operation it has no effect on the overall algorithm performance and therefore allow efficient incremental processing. Second, our experiments showed good results with a simple "binning" and therefore we had no need to use more advanced methods. We discuss the details on the "binning" preprocessing for each variable type below.

Continuous variables

To represent a continuous variable in the cube approach, we need to categorize it into buckets (bins), a process which is referred to as "binning". The simplest way to create these bins is to split the range of all possible values for a variable into equal-sized bins, say using quartiles, quintiles, deciles or any other appropriate percentile.

Assume a continuous variable x with minimum value of x_{min} and maximum value of x_{max} that we want to divide into n equal bins. The boundaries of these bins are given as follows:

$$[x_{min}, x_{min+} \frac{x_{max} - x_{min}}{n}] ,$$

$$[x_{min+} \frac{x_{max} - x_{min}}{n} +1, x_{min+} \frac{x_{max} - x_{min}}{n} * 2],$$

.... ,

$$[x_{min+} \frac{x_{max} - x_{min}}{n} * (n-1), x_{max}]$$

For example, dividing an income variable in the range of 0-10000 into 10 equal-sized bins, results in following bins: 0-1000; 1001-2000, ... , 9001-10000.

In this work, we always use equal size bins to handle continuous variables.

The binning process requires that we know the minimum and maximum values of the variable, which should be pretty straightforward to calculate for the original data. But this may not be as straightforward for incremental data.

Ordinal variables with many values (chi-square binning)

To create cubes from an ordinal variable with many values, we need to collapse "similar" values of the variable into one bin. A common solution to this problem is to use chi-square test for similarity. The number of possible groupings for a variable with many values could be very big. So in this work we use an algorithm that successively combines "pairs" of the variable values, as follows:

For each legitimate pair of the variable values calculate the Chi square and the corresponding P-value.

1.   Chi-square $= \sum \frac{(E-O)^2}{E}$, where O are the observed samples and the E are the expected values.

2.   Find the pair with the max P-value

3.   Combine the two categories with the max P-value provided that the max P-value is smaller than the level of significance ("alpha").

4.   Treat the combined values as one category and return to Step 1.

Note that in the case of an ordinal variable, only adjacent values could be grouped together in order to maintain the ordinal nature of the variable. This reduces the number of "legitimate" pairs to group significantly.

The algorithm described above can only be used in case of predictive models (where there is a dependent variable). In other cases, like clustering algorithms, following algorithms can be used:

1.   Sort the values

2.   Merge similar values (close to each other) into bins

3.   Continue merging until the number of needed bins is created

Ordinal variables with few values

In the case of a discrete or ordinal variable with few values, things are simple, because each value constitutes one segment on that dimension.

For example: If the dataset contains a socio-economic variables with three possible values (high, medium and low), then it can be represented by means of 3 segments on that dimension.

Nominal variables

Binning a nominal variable that has many possible values is similar to the case of an ordinal variable above, except that the number of "legitimate" pairs to consider in the Chi-square test for similarity is much larger (because any attribute value could be grouped with any other attribute value)..

An example is occupation code, which can contain lots of nominal values.

Another possibility to handle nominal variables with many possible values (or any other variable) is to use domain knowledge in order to reduce the number of possible values. For example, occupation can be collapsed into "white color" or "blue color", zip codes can be collapsed based on the first two digits, creating only 100 possible values, each adding being a new segment on the zip code dimension.

Binary variables

Binary variables are the simplest to handle, as no initial preprocessing is required, with each variable is easily converted into two segments on the binary dimension.

Min max scaling

Some algorithms in data mining require that variables (mostly continuous) will be scaled prior to using the algorithm. An example is the K-Means algorithm for clustering which require that all variable will be in the same scale, e.g., between 0 and 1, or otherwise the algorithm yields wrong results. In this work, we consider two transformations for scaling variables: min-max scaling and standardization.

The min-max transformation coverts a variable to lie between given min and max values. The transformation yielding this is:

$$v' = \frac{v - min}{max - min}(max' - min') + min'$$

Where

v is the existing attribute value, with its *min* and *max* values

v' is the new attribute value, with its *min'* and *max'* values

For example, suppose we have a variable with the minimum value of 0 and the maximum value of 5 and we need to be converted into a new variable with minimum of 0 and maximum of 10. The conversion formula for this case is:

$$v' = \frac{v - 0}{5 - 0}(10 - 0) + 0 = v * 2$$

In cases were a set of samples needs to be processed, then a matrix representation of the equation described above, is used:

$$\overline{v}' = \frac{\overline{v} - \overline{min}}{\overline{max} - \overline{min}}(\overline{max'} - \overline{min'}) + \overline{min'}$$

Where:

$\overline{v}$ is a vector of N existing values

$\overline{min}$ is a vector of size 1xN of the N attributes, each with the existing minimum value

$\overline{max}$ is a vector of size 1xN of the N attributes, each with the existing maximum value

$\overline{min'}$ is a vector of size 1xN of the N attributes, each with the new minimum value

$\overline{max'}$ is a vector of size 1xN of the N attributes, each with the new maximum value

$\overline{v'}$ is a vector of the N new attributes

After the min-max conversion has been performed, one applies the binning processed on the transformed variables for representing by means of the cube approach.

Standardization

Another well known scaling technique for continuous variables is standardization. In this case, the variables values are scaled based on their averages and standard deviations, using the equation:

$$v' = \frac{v - avg}{std}$$

When

v is the existing value,

avg is the average value of v

std is the standard deviation of v

v' is the new value.

The standardization transformation can reduce the number of cubes needed in order to represent continuous variables and makes different variables comparable.

Just like in the min-max case this transformation can also be used in a matrix format in order to process a set of samples. In this case the transformation equation is:

$$v' = \frac{v - avg}{std}$$

When

v is a vector of N existing values,

avg is a 1xN vector of the average values,

std is a 1xN vector of the standard deviation,

v' is the vector of the new values

5.3.2 Incremental Pre-Processing

In the incremental approach for data mining, when new observations arrive, the initial preprocessing has already been done and cubes have already been created. However, these new observations might change the variable characteristics (e.g., the min and the max value) which might affect not only the variable representation in the multi dimensional cube, but also the structure of the whole multi dimensional cube.

For example, assume a continuous variable in the range 1-10,000, which is binned into 10 equal segments of size 1000 each. This variable adds 10 dimension to the multi dimensional cube. Now assume that a new observation arrives with a value of 20,000. The question is which dimension in the multi dimensional cube this new point should be assigned to? This is not simple as the existing multi dimensional cube was built to accommodate only variable values in the range of 1-10,000. The purpose of the incremental preprocessing is, among the rest, to resolve this issue.

The incremental pre-processing flow is as follow:
1. Create the pre-processing rules based on the existing data
2. Pre-process all the existing data
3. For each batch of new samples that has been processed,
    a. Check that the statistical parameters used to create the pre-processing rules are still valid
    b. If not, create new pre-processing rules, and pre-process again all the existing data.

We now apply this procedure to the transformations described above.

Continuous variables

To create bins for continuous variables, one needs to know the minimum and maximum values of the variable. The process of updating those bins is:
- When new samples with values larger then the maximum / smaller then the minimum arrive, group several of the existing segments into one (as needed) and create new segments for the new values.
- Follow this process for all new samples, while ensuring that the number of existing segments does not exceed n.

To demonstrate this approach, let's use the example above of a continuous variable in the range 1-10,000 split into 10 equal-sized segments (bins), 0-1000; 1001-2000, ... , 9001-

10000. Now let's assume that we process three batches of new data.

The first dataset with a maximum value for the attribute of 2500, the second with a maximum value of 250, and the third with a maximum value of 20000. Clearly, the first and the second datasets fall within the dimension of the existing multi dimensional cubes so that each point can be assigned to the appropriate dimension without having to modify the multi dimensional cube. Third dataset is problematic, because the maximum value for the attribute exceeds the one used to build the multi dimensional cubes, so in order to maintain the same number of bins, ones required to update the bins sizes accordingly. We do this as follows:

- Merge two adjacent cubes into one cube, thus creating the cubes: 0-2000, 2000-4000, ..., 8000-10000. The number of samples in each segment should be the sum of the number of samples in the "old" segments. For example, the number of samples in the "new" segment 0-2000 should be the number of sample in the "old" segment 0-1000 plus the number of samples in the "old" segment 1000-2000.

- Create the additional dimensions to "fill up the gap" 10001-12000, 12001-14000, ... , 18001-20000.

- With the new segment, the sample that has a maximum value of 20000 can be easily represented.

A more complex case can arise when the newly created segments can not be created exactly from the merging two adjacent segments. For example, if in the sample described above the maximum value of the third dataset was 15,000 (and not 20,000) then the updated segments are: 1-1500,1501-3000, etc. Unlike in the previous case, the new segments overlap the old segments and as a result the original segments can not simply be merged to create the new segments and therefore a slightly different method is needed in order to create the new segments. We use a procedure which is based on the assumption that the data in each cube of the multi-dimensional histogram is uniformly distributed [74, 75], and create the new segments by adding prorated number of data samples from the relevant segments. In the above example, the number of samples in the "new" segment 1-1500 is obtained by adding the number of data samples in the "old" segment 0-1000 plus half of the data samples in the "old" segment 1000-2000. A similar process is followed for all other segments. This way, we can restructure the multi dimensional cube to accommodate the new data without having to rebuild the multi dimensional cube from scratch (which would require scanning the entire dataset again).

Min max scaling

The min-max scaling transforms data samples into a new min-max range. Just like in the previous case, this transformation is also based on knowing in advance the minimum and maximum values of the attribute that needs to be transformed, but in case of incremental processing this knowledge does not necessarily exist. We use the following procedure to update the multi dimensional cube in this case:

- o For each set of new samples, check the maximum and minimum value of the relevant attribute.
- o If the maximum (minimum) value of the attribute in the incremental dataset is larger (smaller) than the maximum (minimum) value for the original dataset, then:
    - i. Update the transformation rule according to the new values
    - ii. Re-process all the existing samples using the new transformation (using the transformation matrix representation)

We demonstrate with a simple example:

Assume that the minimum value of a given attribute in the existing dataset is 0 and the maximum is 5 and that we want to transform this attribute to assume a minimum value 0 and maximum value 10. As shown above, the required transformation is:

$$v' = \frac{v - min}{max - min}(max' - min') + min'$$

$$v' = \frac{v - 0}{5 - 0}(10 - 0) + 0 = \frac{v * 10}{5} = v * 2$$

Now let's consider that the first set of incremental data contain only two observations: 4.85, 0.82. In this case, there is no sample with maximum higher then 5 or minimum lower then 0 so no change in the transformation formula above is needed. Using the matrix representation described above, the modified attribute values are:

$$v' = \begin{bmatrix} 4.85 \\ 0.82 \end{bmatrix} * 2 = \begin{bmatrix} 9.7 \\ 1.64 \end{bmatrix}$$

The second set of samples contains the values: 13.42, 7.35 , 3.5

In this case the maximum value is 13.42 with exceeds the maximum value used so far. Therefore, we need to update the transformation rule, as follows:

$$v' = \frac{v - min}{max - min}(max' - min') + min'$$

$$v' = \frac{v - 0}{13.42 - 0}(10 - 0) + 0 = \frac{v * 10}{13.42} = \frac{v}{1.342}$$

Now we apply this transformation to all the five new observations to yield:

$$v' = \begin{bmatrix} 4.85 \\ 0.82 \\ 13.42 \\ 7.35 \\ 3.5 \end{bmatrix} / 1.342 = \begin{bmatrix} 3.61 \\ 0.61 \\ 10 \\ 5.47 \\ 2.6 \end{bmatrix}$$

When these results are then stored in 10 segments (for example), the results are:

Cube num	Segment range	Number of points in the cube
1	0-1	1
2	1.01-2	0
3	2.01-3	1
4	3.01-4	1
5	4.01-5	0
6	5.01-6	1
7	6.01-7	0
8	7.01-7	0

| 9 | 8.01-9 | 0 |
| 10 | 9.01-10 | 1 |

Table 5 : Cube results for the min-max transformation sample

Standardization

Standardization is a pre-processing transformation based on the average and standard deviation of the samples. This type of transformation is dealt in a similar manner to the previous one. The algorithm is as follows:

- For each set of new samples, update the values of the average and standard deviation.
- Update the transformation rule according to the new values
- Re-process all the existing samples using the new transformation (using the transformation matrix representation)

We again demonstrate with an example:

Assume that the existing dataset contains two observations with one attribute with values 3 and 5, respectively. The average is 4 and the STD is 1.41. The initial transformation is therefore:

$$v' = \frac{v - avg}{std} = \frac{v - 4}{1.41}$$

Yielding the following modified values for the attribute:

$$v' = \frac{\begin{bmatrix} 3 \\ 5 \end{bmatrix} - \begin{bmatrix} 4 \\ 4 \end{bmatrix}}{1.41} = \begin{bmatrix} -0.7 \\ 0.7 \end{bmatrix}$$

Now, the first set of new incremental data contains two samples with attribute values: 4.85, 0.82. We proceed following the algorithm above:

- Update the average and the STD. The new average is 3.55 and the new STD is 2.37
- Update the transformation rule to yield:

$$v' = \frac{v - avg}{std} = \frac{v - 3.55}{2.37}$$

- Re-process all the data samples using the new transformation. The new values are:

$$v' = \frac{\begin{bmatrix} 3 \\ 5 \\ 4.85 \\ 0.82 \end{bmatrix} - \begin{bmatrix} 3.55 \\ 3.55 \\ 3.55 \\ 3.55 \end{bmatrix}}{2.37} = \begin{bmatrix} -0.23 \\ 0.61 \\ 0.54 \\ -1.15 \end{bmatrix}$$

Binning using chi-square test

The chi-square test is used in order to find the best possible bins for an attribute. When new samples arrive, the original bins are likely to change and need to be updated. But since updating the bins for each new sample requires a lot of processing resources, we set up a threshold such that if this threshold is met, the chi-square test is applied on all observations to calculate the new bins and restructure the new multi dimensional space. Otherwise, if this threshold is not met, we still use the existing bins and assign the new observations to the existing multi dimensional cube. This threshold can be expressed by means of the number of samples processed since the last bin update, the difference in the chi-square values, or others.

The algorithm to update the chi square values in light of new observations is fully explained in the classification chapter and therefore not described here.

This binning process applies to both nominal and ordinal variables with multiple values. In the case nominal and ordinal variables with fewer values, we proceed as follows.

Few Discrete Values

As long as the set of discrete values for the new observations are the same as for existing observations, there is no change in the structure of the multi dimensional cube.

Whenever a new value appears, we may handle it in one of these two ways:

- Combine the new value into one of the existing segments.
- Merge two of the existing segments into one segment and creating a new segment for the new value.

The best solution to implement depends on the situation at hand. If the new value is similar to one of the existing ones, then merging them together is appropriate. If the new value is a completely different value, then creating a new segment may be more preferable.

Binary variables

Finally, no special action is required to deal with binary variables.

5.4 Conclusion

This section has analyzed the manner in which the pre-processing rules need to be updated whenever new samples arrive. We are concerned here with preprocessing required for building and modifying the multi dimensional cube, and not with the "conventional" preprocessing required to prepare the dataset for mining. We distinguish between the initial preprocessing and the incremental preprocessing. The initial preprocessing is invoked for the first batch of data (the "original" data) to build the multi dimensional cube, whereas the incremental preprocessing is invoked for any set of incremental data to update and modify the multi dimensional cube.

We next proceed to describe the DMEF non-profit dataset used in this work and the pre-processing applied on this file to prepare it for incremental data mining.

6 Implementation on the DMEF Non-Profit Dataset

6.1 Dataset Description

We use a relatively large real life dataset to test the cube-based approach for knowledge update and compare its performance against non-incremental algorithms applied on the entire dataset. This dataset was made available for research by the Direct Marketing Educational Foundation (DMEF).

The file was originated from a non-profit organization that uses direct mail to solicit additional contributions from previous donors. The response variable is binary: 1 if a donor responded to the solicitation offer, 0 otherwise. The objective of the model is to predict the response probability.

The dataset which was provided by DMEF was a relatively "clean" subset of the actual mailing campaign including 99,200 observations, of which 27,208 were responders, with 77 variables for each observation. We refer to this file below as the non-profit file.

Several transformations were made to the non-profit file for modeling purposes:
a. Dates were converted to the number of days from a specific reference date (the number of days since the customer entered the database).
b. The continuous variables were converted to categorical variables using binning.
c. Zip codes were converted to categorical variables, using binning, according to the first two digits.
d. Variables with more than 5% of values missing were excluded.
e. When the number of observations with missing values for an attribute was less then 5%, the missing values were replaced by 0's and a dummy variable was added for each such attribute to "capture" the missing value effect, assuming a value of 1 if the attribute has a missing value, 0 otherwise.
f. Numeric predictors were truncated if their values exceeded $6*\sigma$ from the average. This transformation was not applied to binary variables.

93

This preprocessing has increased the number of predictors in the non-profit file from the original 77 variables to 307 variables, 273 of them binary and the others continuous. The list of the original variables and their complete transformations can be found in the Appendix.

To evaluate the incremental approach for knowledge update, we have split the dataset randomly into a training dataset, containing 50,000 observations, and a validation dataset containing the remaining of the observations. The training dataset was further split randomly into two sub-groups: a set of 40,000 samples to create the initial model, and a set of "new" 10,000 observations to incrementally update the model. The resulting model was then validated against the validation dataset.

The incremental approach for knowledge update was also compared to the results of the corresponding non-incremental approach. In this case, we used the entire training dataset (of 50,000 samples) for building the (non-incremental) model, validating it against the validation dataset.

Hence, the validation process of both the incremental and non-incremental approach for knowledge update was conducted on the same validation dataset. This brings all models onto the same footing for comparison purposes. For the most part, only the results corresponding to the validation dataset will be presented below.

6.2 Building the Multi Dimensional Cube to Represent the Non Profit File

We used the approach describe above to build the multi-dimensional cube to represent the non profit file. First, applying the initial preprocessing on the original training dataset of 40,000 observations, and then the incremental preprocessing algorithm to modify the multi-dimensional cubes to accommodate the incremental 10, 000 observations. In total, 37,980 cubes were needed in order to represent the entire dataset.

6.3 Upper Bound on the Number of Cubes

As mentioned above, the non-profit data file contains 307 variables, of which 273 are binary and 34 are continuous. So an interesting issue is what is what is the upper bound on the number of cubes to store this dataset?

If we assume 10 bins per continuous variable and, of course, 2 bins per binary variable, then, theoretically, the number of cubes required to store the data is $10^{34} * 2^{273} = 1.5 * 10^{116}$. This represents far too many cubes. But given the properties of multi-dimensional databases discussed in Chapter 3, we show that the number of cubes needed is much lower, by an order of magnitude. Even this estimate is an upper bound on the number of cubes as the actual number of cubes is in fact much smaller than the upper bound. In estimating the number of cubes, we follow the steps described in chapter 3.

Step #1 – Data pre-processing

We started with a "conventional" preprocessing of the data, to clean up the data, primarily eliminating from the dataset "weak" predictors, namely attributes for which more than 99.5% of the values were identical. We also eliminated predictors which are highly correlated with the each other (absolute correlation level of .70 or above). Correlated variables are two or more variables which represent similar information, and therefore at least one of them is not needed. Since the non-profit dataset was a relatively clean set, only 18 binary variables s were eliminated in the preprocessing step, reducing the number of variables to 289 attributes – 34 continuous variables and 255 binary variables.

Step #2 – Handling the binary variables

As discussed in Chapter 3, to save space, binary variables (for each observation) are represented by the location vector. For example: the binary attribute vector (0,1,0,0,1,0,0) is represented by the location vector (2,5). Note that this representation changed the predictors from binary to ordinal.

Now, the maximum number of 'ones' in any observation, turned out to be 28. This effectively reduces the number predictors from 253 binary predictors to only 28 ordinal predictors. In Figure 20 we present the distribution of the number of observations as a function of the number of ordinal predictors in the location vectors. For example, there were approximately 2500 observations with three location attributes (meaning that only three predictors were 'ones', all of the rest were zero), approximately 6200 observations with 5 location attributes, etc.

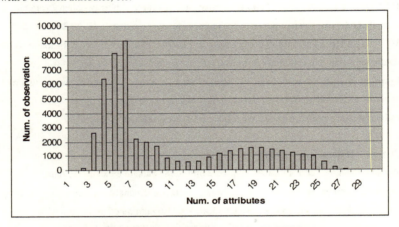

Figure 19 : Distance distribution on the DMEF dataset

From figure 20, we can see that only 20 attributes are needed to represent more than 90% of the observations.

Step #3 – Handling the continuous variables

Step#3a – binning the continuous variables

We recall that there are 34 continuous variables in the dataset. Each one of these variables was binned into 10 equally-sized bins. For example, a continuous variable in the range 1-100 is binned into 10 bins (segments) each of size 10, i.e., 1-10, 11-20, and so on. To render only "significant" bins, we combined bins which contained less than 5% of the observations with the adjacent bins. This converted the 34 continuous variables into 34 ordinal variables.

Step #3b – binning ordinal variables

The previous step converted 273 binary variables in 20 ordinal variables. These new 20 variables were also binned into 10 equally sized bins, combining, as above, adjacent bins that contain less then 5% of the observations.

Step #4 – Finding the estimated number of cubes

Combining the number of variables from Step 3a and 3b yields altogether 54 ordinal variables to represent the original dataset. The actual number of bins needed for each variable is described in the following table:

Num. of Bins	Num. of dimensions
2	33
3	4
4	3
5	3
6	3
7	4
8	2
9	1
11	1

Table 6 : Number of bins for each dimension

Namely, there are 33 variables that actually need 2 bins, 4 variables the need 3 bins, etc.

Based on this table, the upper bound for the number of cubes is given by multiplying the number of bins for all the variables, i.e.:

Upper bound on the number of cubes = $\prod_{i=1}^{9} b_i^{n_i}$

where b_i is the number of bins in the ith row of the table above
and n_i is the number of dimensions in the ith row of the table

In this case, the upper bound on the number of cubes is $2^{33}*3^{4}*...*11^{1} = 1.8*10^{24}$

While this upper bound is still very large, it is nevertheless much smaller than the theoretical upper bound estimate of $1.5 * 10^{116}$ cubes. But even this approach yields an upper bound level which is much too high. In practice, however, this upper bound is irrelevant as most of the cubes are still empty. To find an estimate of the number of cubes which are actually occupied, we pursue the simulation approach suggested in Chapter 3.

6.4 Estimating the Actual Number of Cubes to Store the Data

As mentioned in Chapter 3, we estimate the number of cubes needed to store the data, by applying the cube-based approach on a sample of customers taken randomly from the dataset and then expanding that number based on the ratio m/n, where n is the size of the sample and m the number of cubes required.

In our case, we selected a sample of 10,000 observations from the non-profit database. 6,817 cubes were required to store this sample in the cube approach, using 2 bins to represent each binary variable and 10 bins for each continuous variable. The expansion factor is: $\dfrac{6,817}{10,000} = 0.6817$

Using this ratio, the estimated number of non empty cubes required to store the entire training set of 50,000 observations, is;

$$0.6817 * 50,000 = 34,085$$

We recall that the actual number of cubes required to represent the entire training dataset was 37,980, not far from the estimate of 34,085. Considering that we were able to reach approximately 90% of the actual number of cubes required with such a simple process, the results are quite acceptable.

6.5 Comparing the Original and the Cube Representation of the Data

One of the key issues that we need to analyze is how different is the cube-based representation of the data from the original dataset? This has an important impact on the quality of the models based on the cube-based approach. Large deviations between the two datasets might deteriorate the quality of the models as compared to the original ones. We analyze this issue in this section for our non profit file, using the following procedure:

1. For each variable in the training dataset find the minimum value, maximum value, mean and STD.
2. Construct and populate the multi dimensional cube, based on these statistics
3. For each variable in the converted data set find the minimum value, maximum value, mean and STD using the cube data
4. Compare the results of step#1 and step#3

For all the binary variables the STD and the mean were exactly the same for the original data and the cube data – as expected.

For the continuous predictors the difference was minimal, as described in detail in Appendix 3. To summarize there results,

- The maximum difference in the STD between the original data and the cube data was 1.4. This difference has occurred in 2 (out of 307) variables.
- The maximum change in the STD was 4. This difference occurred in 4 (out of 307) attributes
- The average difference in the mean between the original data and the cube data is 0.15
- The average difference in the STD between the original data and the cube data is 0.036.

These results clearly show that the difference between the original values and the cube-based values are very minor, suggesting that there the cube-based model should be significantly different than models based on the original dataset. We investigate this phenomenon in the next chapters, when we apply various data mining algorithms on the original dataset and the cube-based dataset and compare the results.

6.6 Sensitivity Analysis for the Memory Usage of the Cubes

One of the main advantages of using the cube-based dataset instead of the actual data is the saving in memory required to store the data samples.

.

To store the original data, the amount of memory required is

$$\text{Mem}_{\text{original}} = \text{Number of Samples} * \text{Number of attributes per sample}$$

We recall that in the cube-based representation of the data, we save only the cube number (that implies on its location) and the number of data points inside this cube. Therefore, the amount of memory needed is

$$\text{Mem}_{\text{cubes}} = 2*\text{Number of Cubes that contain samples}$$

We multiply the number of cubes by 2 because we need to save the location of the cube (the cube's number), which is 1 byte long, and the number of data points in this cube, an additional 1 byte for each cube.

This is under the assumption that the number of data points in each cube is "small" enough so it can be accommodated only in one byte.

A simple sensitivity analysis was performed to show the relation between the memory requirements to store the original sample points and the cube-based points, as a function of the number of samples for the non profit dataset. The results are presented in Table 7 and graphically in Figure 21.

Num. of Samples	Num. of cubes	Samples memory	Cubes memory
50,000	37,980	15,300,000	75,960
40,000	28,428	12,240,000	56,856
30,000	18,433	9,180,000	36,866
20,000	12,241	6,120,000	24,482

100

| 10,000 | 6,817 | 3,060,000 | 13,634 |

Table 7 : Sensitivity analysis for the cubes memory usage

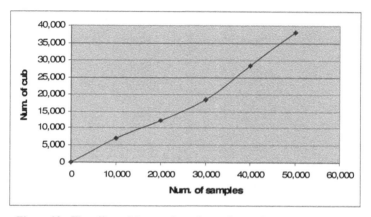

Figure 20 : The effect of the number of samples on the number of cubes

From these results we can clearly see that using the cubes can save approximately 99% of the storage space required to store the original dataset.

Note that the predicted number of cubes that was required to represent 50,000 observations, according to section 2 above, was 32,340. When the actual data was processed the actual number of cubes used was 37,980. We can see that the initial estimate was quite good.

Another experiment that we performed on the same dataset is to explore the effect of number of dimensions on the number of cubes. For this sake, we created cubes using different number of dimensions on the training dataset of the non profit file (50,000 observations). The results are summarized Table 8 and graphically in Figure 22:

Num. of dimensions	Num. of cubes

50	206
100	32,658
150	33,561
200	34,108
269	37,980

Table 8 : Sensitivity analysis for the number of dimensions on the cubes

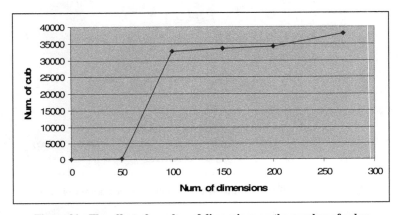

Figure 21 : The effect of number of dimensions on the number of cubes

When the number of dimensions is smaller then 100, then we can see a large increase in the number of cubes as the number of dimensions increases. When the number of dimensions is larger then 100, then the increase in the number of cubes is not nearly as steep as in the earlier case.

6.7 Calibrating the Number of Cubes

The crucial issue we encounter when implementing the cube-based approach for data representation, is to determine the actual bins size. This is especially critical for continuous variables, as the number of bins is the number of segments created on this dimension. To find the "optimal" number of bins in this case, we use the following algorithm:

- Create a small calibration dataset from the training set

102

- Create the model (linear regression, classification, etc.) based on calibration dataset, to be used as our target model
- Decide on the size of the bin (could be quite large at first) and create the multi dimensional cube to store the data
- Run the data mining model on the cube-based dataset
- If the results of the cube-based model are good enough in comparison with the target model, then stop
- Otherwise, create smaller bins and repeat the process

This iterative process will allow us to calibrate the size of the cubes to the point where the model created from the cubes data is very similar to the model created form the original data.

6.8 Conclusions

This chapter described the heuristic model to estimate the number of cubes required to store a given data set. The model is based on the property discussed above that multi dimensional cubes are sparsely populated therefore allowing us to represent a dataset with fewer dimensions. Based on the number of dimensions and the distribution of the data in these dimensions, the number of needed cubes can be estimated.
The model was implemented on the non-profit dataset with very good results, with the expected number of cubes being similar to the actual number of cubes.
In addition, we show that by representing our data by means of the cube-based approach, we can save a lot of memory.

In the following chapters, we describe the application of our incremental data mining approach for various data mining models.

7 Linear Regression

7.1 Introduction

Regression is a way to understand the relationship between several independent variables and a dependent variable. Perhaps the most important application of regression analysis is to predict the value of the dependent variable for given values of the independent variables. Examples of regression problems are: predicting the chance that a patient has a certain disease given the results of several medical tests; predicting the demand for a certain product given its characteristics and its promotion history; predicting stock prices in the future given the market behavior in the past and macroeconomic characteristics, among others. In fact, regression analysis, in all its forms, is perhaps the most commonly used statistical model. There are many forms of regression, depending upon the relationships between the dependent and independent variables and the type of the dependent and independent variables involved. . The most basic model is the linear regression model which applies to the case where the dependent variable is linearly related to the independent variables.

In this chapter we describe a cube-based algorithm for incremental linear regression. We apply this algorithm to the non-profit dataset described above and compare the results to those obtained with the non-incremental linear regression algorithm.

7.2 The Linear Regression Model

The general linear regression model is given by the expression:

$$y = \beta_0 + \beta_1 x_1 + \beta_2 x_2 + ... + \beta_n x_n + \varepsilon$$

Where:

$x_1, x_2, ..., x_n$ are the independent variables

$\beta_0, \beta_1, \beta_2, ..., \beta_n$ are the corresponding coefficients

y is the dependent variable

ε is the random error

For simplicity, we ignore the observation index here.

Since the coefficients β_i's are not known, they need to be estimated based on sample data. The sample regression model is given by the expression:

$$\hat{y} = b_0 + b_1 x_1 + b_2 x_2 + ... + b_n x_n$$

Where $b_0, b_1, b_2, ..., b_n$ are the coefficient estimates and $\hat{y}$ is the estimated y value.

These coefficients are estimated using the method of least squares [9].

Using matrix notation, the linear regression model is represented by the equation [9];

$$Y = X * \beta + \varepsilon$$

where:

β is the coefficients vector $\beta = \begin{pmatrix} \beta_0 \\ \beta_1 \\ .. \\ \beta_n \end{pmatrix}$

Y is the dependent variable vector $Y = \begin{pmatrix} y_1 \\ ... \\ y_n \end{pmatrix}$

X is the matrix of data points (independents) $X = \begin{pmatrix} 1 & x_{1,1} & \cdots & x_{n,1} \\ 1 & \cdots & & \\ 1 & & & \\ 1 & x_{1,m} & \cdots & x_{n,m} \end{pmatrix}$

and ε is the error vector $\varepsilon = \begin{pmatrix} \varepsilon_1 \\ \cdots \\ \varepsilon_n \end{pmatrix}$

The first column in the matrix X corresponds to the intercept of the line and is therefore all 1's, each of the other columns are the data points.

The sample regression line is given by $\hat{Y} = X * B$, where B is the corresponding vector estimate given by [4]:

$$B = (X'X)^{-1} X'Y.$$

It can be shown that the linear model holds if the following four conditions are true;

1. The expected value of the random errors, for any given value of the independent variable, is 0.
2. The variance of the random errors is a constant, for all values of x.
3. The distribution of the random errors is normal.
4. The errors associated with any two observations are independent.

However, it is not required that each of these conditions are met for the linear model to hold true. Some of these conditions are required for testing hypotheses about the quality of the estimation results. For further details, see [9].

The accuracy measure which is usually used to assess how well the linear regression line fits the data is the R-square, which describes the fraction of the variability explained by the explanatory variable, X. R-Square is a measure between 0 and 1. The larger the value of R-square and the closer it is to one, the more variability is explained by the model, and the better the fit. And vice versa, the lower the value of R-square and the closer it is to zero, the weaker is the fit. Statistical tests, involving t-tests and F-tests, are available to test the significance of the R-square value and the coefficient estimates [9].

7.3 Evaluation Criteria

R-Square values measure the overall accuracy of the model, the higher the R-square values, the more accurate the fit of the model to the data. In business applications, we may be more interested in the quality of the model than its accuracy. For example, in database marketing applications, the R-square of the regression model is usually very small, often less than 10%. Should one attempt to improve the R-square value by even percentage point or two, they may run into an over-fitting problem. What is more important in these types of applications is how the model affects profitability and whether it yields stable results. These are not measured by R-square values but by other measures which are discussed below. These measures apply, perhaps with some variations, to all types of predictive modeling in data mining.

In this work, we apply the linear regression model on a binary dependent variable. Consequently, we present these measures for binary models, where the dependent variable assumes the value of 1 ("responder") and zero ("non-responder"). Equivalent measures also exist for "true" linear regression models where the dependent variable is continuous [77].

- **Gain charts** -
  Gains chart display the incremental "lift" obtained by the model, versus the null model that assumes that all customers are the same.
  The X axis represents the cumulative proportion of the population,
  $X_i = 100 * 1/n$.

The Y axis represents the cumulative percentage of the actual response (e.g., the proportion of buyers),

$$Y_i = 100 * \sum_{j=1}^{i} y_j \bigg/ \sum_{j=1}^{n} y_j$$

where the observations are ordered such that $\hat{y}_i \leq \hat{y}_{i+1}$ (see Figure below).

The 45 degrees straight line emanating from the origin exhibits the null model, the curve above it, and the model results. The distance between the model results and the null model results is the gain in response, also known as the lift, which is attained by the model at that point.

- **The Gini Coefficient** [77] –

    The area between the model curve and the null model (the gray area in the Figure below) divided by the area below the null model (the white triangle area in figure below), is defined as the Gini coefficient.

    A large Gini coefficient value indicates, for most problems, a better model.

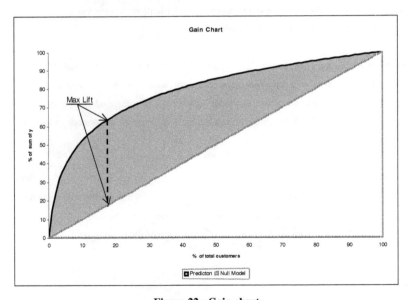

Figure 22 : Gain chart

108

Lorenz Curve –

The Lorenz curve was described in [78] as a graphical representation of income distribution. The difference between the Gain chart and the Lorenz curve are the values along the y axis. While in gain charts the y-axis represents the cumulative % response, in the Lorenz curve, the y axis represents the cumulative % income (or profit). When two models creates similar Lorenz Curves (the distance between the two curves is very small for the entire range of values) this is an indication that the two models are more-or-less the same, and vice-versa.

- **Kolmogorov-Smirnov test (KS-test)**

The Kolmogorov-Smirnov (KS) statistic is the maximum lift between the null model and the regression model, as shown in the gains chart above.

The KS test [80] is a statistical test to determine if the KS statistic is significant. Should it be, this is an indication that the two distributions, one given by the null model and the other by the regression model, are significantly different. The KS-test is a non-parametric, distribution free test, defined by:

H_0:	The data follow a specified distribution
H_1:	The data do not follow the specified distribution
Test Statistic:	The Kolmogorov-Smirnov test statistic is defined as

$$D = \max_{1 \leq i \leq N} \left| F(Y_i) - \frac{i}{N} \right|$$

where F is the theoretical cumulative distribution of the distribution being tested.

Significance Level: $\alpha = 5\%$

In our case, H_0 will be that the regression results and the null model are distributed similarly, and H_1 will be that the regression results and the null model have a different distribution.

The hypothesis regarding the distributional form H_0 is rejected if the test statistic, D, is greater than the critical value obtained from a table.

7.4 The Analytical Incremental Linear Regression

In the case of linear regression, one can establish an efficient analytical method of updating the model's parameter estimates when new data arrives, without having to start the algorithm from scratch. We describe this algorithm in is this section.

As discussed in the previous chapters, the main problem with the analytical incremental algorithms is defining the internal quantities that one needs to preserve from the previous model in order to update the model when new data arrive, without slowing down the algorithm considerably or consuming a great deal of memory.

Recall that the coefficient estimate of a linear regression model is given by:

$$B = (X'X)^{-1} X'Y$$

The internal values that need to be saved in this case are:

- $X'X$
- $X'Y$

Both are matrices which can be updated easily with additional observations

Denoting:

n – the number of processed samples.

m – the number of new samples (that need to be processed).

d – the problem's dimension (the number of attributes in each sample).

X_i - the X matrix after processing i samples

Before processing the new samples:

$$X_n = \begin{pmatrix} 1 & \cdots & x_{n,1} \\ \cdots & & \cdots \\ 1 & \cdots & x_{n,d} \end{pmatrix}$$

$$X'_n X_n = \begin{pmatrix} 1 & \cdots & 1 \\ \cdots & & \cdots \\ x_{n,1} & \cdots & x_{n,d} \end{pmatrix} \begin{pmatrix} 1 & \cdots & x_{n,1} \\ \cdots & & \cdots \\ 1 & \cdots & x_{n,d} \end{pmatrix} = \begin{pmatrix} 1*d & x_{n,1}+\ldots+x_{n,d} \\ x_{n,1}+\ldots+x_{n,d} & x_{n,1}^2+\ldots+x_{n,d}^2 \end{pmatrix}$$

After processing the m additional samples, we get:

$$X_{n+m} = \begin{pmatrix} 1 & \cdots & x_{n,1} & x_{n+1,1} & \cdots & x_{n+m,1} \\ \cdots & & \cdots & \cdots & & \cdots \\ 1 & \cdots & x_{n,d} & x_{n+1,d} & \cdots & x_{n+m,d} \end{pmatrix}$$

$$X'_{n+m} X_{n+m} = \begin{pmatrix} 1 & \cdots & 1 \\ \cdots & & \cdots \\ x_{n,1} & \cdots & x_{n,d} \\ x_{n+1,1} & \cdots & x_{n+1,d} \\ \cdots & & \cdots \\ x_{n+m,1} & \cdots & x_{n+m,d} \end{pmatrix} \begin{pmatrix} 1 & \cdots & x_{n,1} & x_{n+1,1} & \cdots & x_{n+m,1} \\ \cdots & & \cdots & \cdots & & \cdots \\ 1 & \cdots & x_{n,d} & x_{n+1,d} & \cdots & x_{n+m,d} \end{pmatrix} =$$

$$\begin{pmatrix} 1*d & \cdots & x_{n,1}+\ldots+x_{n,d} & x_{n+1,1}+\ldots+x_{n+1,d} & \cdots & x_{n+m,1}+\ldots+x_{n+m,d} \\ & & \cdots & & & \cdots \\ x_{n,1}+\ldots+x_{n,d} & \cdots & x_{n,1}^2+\ldots+x_{n,d}^2 & x_{n,1}x_{n+1,1}+x_{n,d}x_{n+1,d} & \cdots & x_{n,1}x_{n+m,1}+x_{n,d}x_{n+m,d} \\ x_{n+1,1}+\ldots+x_{n+1,d} & \cdots & x_{n,1}x_{n+1,1}+x_{n,d}x_{n+1,d} & x_{n+1,1}^2+\ldots+x_{n+1,d}^2 & \cdots & x_{n+1,1}x_{n+m,1}+x_{n+1,d}x_{n+m,d} \\ & & & & & \\ x_{n+m,1}+\ldots+x_{n+m,d} & & x_{n,1}x_{n+m,1}+x_{n,d}x_{n+m,d} & x_{n+m,1}x_{n+1,1}+x_{n+m,d}x_{n+1,d} & \cdots & x_{n+m,1}^2+\ldots+x_{n+m,d}^2 \end{pmatrix}$$

This analysis shows that in order to update the matrix with the new m samples, all that is needed is to add the matrix m rows and m columns, whose calculation are relatively simple.

A similar calculation exists for the second parameter (XY).
Before processing the new samples:

$$X_n = \begin{pmatrix} 1 & \dots & x_{n,1} \\ \dots & & \dots \\ 1 & \dots & x_{n,d} \end{pmatrix}$$

$$Y_n = \begin{pmatrix} y_1 \\ \dots \\ y_n \end{pmatrix}$$

$$X_n'Y_n = \begin{pmatrix} 1 & \dots & 1 \\ \dots & & \dots \\ x_{n,1} & \dots & x_{n,d} \end{pmatrix}\begin{pmatrix} y_1 \\ \dots \\ y_n \end{pmatrix} = \begin{pmatrix} y_1 + \dots + y_n \\ \dots \\ x_{n,1}y_1 + \dots + x_{n,d}y_n \end{pmatrix}$$

After adding the m new samples:

$$X_{n+m} = \begin{pmatrix} 1 & \dots & x_{n,1} & x_{n+1,1} & .. & x_{n+m,1} \\ \dots & & \dots & \dots & & \dots \\ 1 & \dots & x_{n,d} & x_{n+1,d} & \dots & x_{n+m,d} \end{pmatrix}$$

$$Y_{n+m} = \begin{pmatrix} y_1 \\ \dots \\ y_n \\ y_{n+1} \\ \dots \\ y_{n+m} \end{pmatrix}$$

$$X_{n+m}'Y_{n+m} = \begin{pmatrix} 1 & \dots & x_{n,1} & x_{n+1,1} & .. & x_{n+m,1} \\ \dots & & \dots & \dots & & \dots \\ 1 & \dots & x_{n,d} & x_{n+1,d} & \dots & x_{n+m,d} \end{pmatrix}\begin{pmatrix} y_1 \\ \dots \\ y_n \\ y_{n+1} \\ \dots \\ y_{n+m} \end{pmatrix} =$$

$$\begin{pmatrix} y_1 + \dots + y_n \\ \dots \\ x_{n,1}y_1 + \dots + x_{n,d}y_n \\ x_{n+1,1}y_1 + \dots + x_{n+1,d}y_{n+1} \\ \dots \\ x_{n+1,1}y_1 + \dots + x_{n+m,d}y_{n+1} \end{pmatrix}$$

Therefore, updating the $X'Y$ when new data arrives is also simple: simply add m rows which are quite painless to calculate.

Having updated these two matrices, as above, one can re-calculate the expression $B = (X'X)^{-1}X'Y$ using the updated matrices to yield the new coefficients.

In sum, the analytical incremental algorithm for linear regression consists of the following steps:

1. Get new samples
2. Update the $X'X$ matrix by adding the required elements to the matrix. No re-calculation of the whole matrix is required
3. Update the $X'Y$ matrix by adding the required elements. No re-calculation of the whole matrix is required
4. Based on the results obtained from step#2, find $(X'X)^{-1}$
5. Based on steps #3 and #4 calculate $B = (X'X)^{-1}X'Y$
6. Return to step #1 to process further samples.

This algorithm solves the problem of incremental linear regression, and allows us to keep the linear regression model up-to-date at all times.

7.5 The Cube-Based Incremental Linear Regression

We now describe the cube-based incremental linear regression algorithm. This algorithm permits us to incrementally update the linear regression model using the cube data.

- Initialization step
  a. Get the boundaries of the problem space for both the dependent and

independent variables. The number of dimensions in the problem space is marked d.

    b. Decide on the size of the cubes (as described in the pre-processing section below).

- Update the relevant cube

    c. Get new data points

    d. For each new data point $(x_{1,n+1}, ..., x_{i,n+1}, ..., x_{d,n+1})$ where $x_{i,j}$ indicates the ith attribute in the jth sample.

        i. Find the cube to which this data point belongs.

        ii. If this cubes has already been used

        then increase the counter for this cube (recall that the data stored for each cube is the number of data points) else create this cube with counter=1

- Update the regression

    e. Create the W matrix from the cubes.

    Based on the model described in chapter 4, the W matrix is created and later used by the regression algorithm. This matrix contains the locations of the cubes that have data points in them.

$$A = \begin{pmatrix} 1 & w_{1,1} & ... & w_{n,1} \\ 1 & ... & & \\ 1 & & & \\ 1 & & & \\ 1 & w_{1,d} & ... & w_{n,d} \end{pmatrix}$$

The matrix should be created according to the following steps:

I. The first column of the matrix is all 1's.

II. For each cube that contains data, create a column with the location of the cube $(w_{i,1}, ..., w_{i,d})$

III. Repeat step II according to the number of data points in this cube.

In this manner, the W matrix is of the same dimension as the original X matrix plus 1 column on 1's, but instead of using the actual data points, the matrix contain the cube values. Note that in cases were there are several data points in the same cube, and then this cube will be represented several times in the W matrix. For example, if a given cube contains 2 data points, then this cube will be represented twice in the W matrix (there will be 2 identical columns).

f. Create a C matrix. The C matrix is a cube representation of the Y matrix, and it has the following format

$$C = \begin{pmatrix} y_1 \\ .. \\ y_n \end{pmatrix}$$

Where y_i is the predicated value for the ith sample.

g. Estimate the regression using;

$$B = (W'W)^{-1}W'C$$

where B is the coefficients vector, C is the predicted values matrix and W is the data matrix based on the cubes. For further explanations on this equation see [4].

• For each new data point that arrives, return to step 2.

7.6 Implementation on the Non Profit Dataset

As mentioned above, while the linear regression model is designed to predict the values of a continuous variable, we apply it to our non-profit data for which the dependent variable is binary Yes/No. This model is referred in the literature as the Linear Probability Model (LPM), because the predicted values of the dependent variable can be interpreted as (purchase) probabilities, $\pi(x)$. There are three main implications of using linear regression for binary dependent variables:

- The linear regression model is not bounded from either above or below. As a results, the predicated probabilities will not be limited to the range of [0,1], in contrast to the basic axiom that probabilities are numbers between 0 and 1. We can "overcome" this issue in our case by setting all negative probabilities to 0 and all probabilities which are greater than one to 1.
- The variance of the error term (ε) is given by the expression $\pi(x)[1 - \pi(x)]$ where $\pi(x)$ is the purchase probability. Since $\pi(x)$ varies from customer to customer.
- Finally the y_i's are binary and therefore can not be normally distributed.

In spite of these limitations, the LPM is widely used in practice because it gives "good" ranking of customers according to their likelihood of purchase.

Consequently, we have chosen to use the non-profit database also for evaluating the linear regression model results. This will also make things consistent with the other chapters, each uses a different data mining model to predict the purchase probabilities.. Finally, we note that the main objective of this work is to evaluate the performance of the cube-based approach for incremental knowledge update, and the LPM seems to be a sufficiently good technique for this.

7.6.1 Original Linear Regression Results

The process of testing the linear regression algorithm on the non-profit dataset involves two steps: First, using GainSmart [80] to choose the set of influential predicators; and second, to run the linear regression algorithm and estimate the model parameters (coefficients). .

Applying the original (non incremental) linear regression algorithm on the original non-profit dataset yield the following measures::

- Training Data
  - R^2: 0.2022
  - Adjusted R^2: 0.2
- Validation Data
  - R^2: 0.1939
- Gains table for the validation dataset at the decile level:

% Customers	Expected response rate	% Response	Actual response rate %
10.0	0.63	30.73	62.29
10.0	0.39	19.46	39.00
10.0	0.27	13.73	27.14
10.0	0.20	10.42	20.54
10.0	0.16	7.14	13.83
10.0	0.13	5.52	9.43
10.0	0.11	4.26	7.07
10.0	0.09	3.38	9.48
10.0	0.05	2.75	5.62
10.0	0.01	2.61	4.92

Table 9 : Linear regression results

7.6.2 Cube-Based Incremental Linear Regression Results

We now apply the linear regression model on the cube-based data. The process involves three steps:

1. Selecting the most influential predictors using GainSmart [80] based on the training dataset containing 40,000 observations and running the linear regression model on the W matrix described above

2. Updating cube-based data to account for the incremental 10,000 new samples and running the linear regression model on the updated W matrix.

3. Validating the incremental model results on a validation dataset that contained 40,000 samples.

The results of the incremental algorithm are:

- Training Data
    - R^2: 0.204
    - Adjusted R^2: 0.2015
- Validation Data
    - R^2: 0.2025
- Gains table for the validation dataset at the decile level:

% Customers	Expected response rate	% Response	Actual response rate %
10	0.64	25.44	64.44
10	0.39	15.78	39.96
10	0.32	11.98	30.34
10	0.29	11.42	28.91
10	0.25	8.57	21.71
10	0.21	7.62	19.29
10	0.18	6.58	16.65
10	0.15	5.21	13.21
10	0.11	4.16	10.52
10	0.05	3.24	8.21

Table 10 : Incremental linear regression validation results

7.7 Results Analysis

7.7.1 Regression Models Comparison

We compared the results for original linear regression model and the cube-based incremental linear regression model by means of several criteria, summarized in Table 11.

	Original Linear regression	"cube-based" incremental Linear Regression
Training R^2	0.2022	0.204
Validation R^2	0.1939	0.2025
Ratio between Training R^2 and Validation R^2	1.04	1.007
Gini Coefficient	0.216074	0.180317

Table 11 : Comparison table for the linear regression model

Comparing the results for the training and validation datasets suggests that there is no over-fitting for either model (since the ratio between the training R^2 and the validation R^2 is approximately 1). In addition, the original linear regression model yields results which are relatively similar to the results obtained by the cube-based incremental linear regression algorithm.

We note in this table that the cube-based approach yields R^2 values that are slightly better than the R^2 values for the original linear regression model, for both the training and the validation dataset. As discussed above in Section 4.3, we attribute this difference to the fact that the cube-based approach for representing data is better able to handle noisy data. This phenomenon is further explained in the next section where we use different cube sizes to build models.

Finally, we present the gain charts for the validation data for both algorithms and the corresponding Lorenz curves.

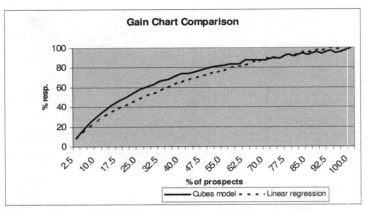

Figure 23 : Gains charts for the linear regression model

Both charts indicate that the two modeling approaches, the original linear regression model which uses the original data and the linear regression model which uses the cube-base data representation, yield very similar results. Therefore, the effect of using cube-based data instead of the actual data is negligible.

The same conclusion is obtained based on the Lorenz Curve for these two algorithms.

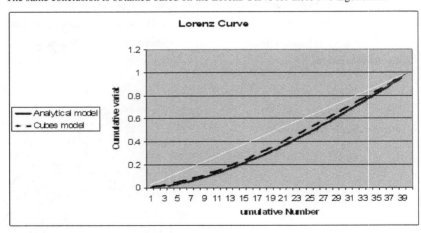

120

Figure 24 : Lorenz curves for the linear regression model

In addition, we used the KS-test to determine if the results of the original data linear regression model and the results of the cube-based model are significantly different from each other. The results of the KS tests were $D=0.1750$ with a corresponding $P=0.531$. This indicates that the results if the two algorithms are not significantly different from each other.

7.7.2 Predictor Comparison

To create the best possible model for each dataset, we ran the specification process, using GainSmart, separately for the original training dataset and for the cube-based training dataset. While the previous sections showed that the results received in both case are very similar, comparing the actual predictors affecting each model can give us additional insight about the model results.

We found that 25 out of 32 predictors that were used in the cube model where also used in the original data mode. This uses as another indication to the similarity between the two models.

7.7.3 Storage Usage Results

One of the major benefits of using the cubes model the savings in storage space needed in order to store the data.

The original linear regression algorithm is based on the X matrix, whose size is a multiplication of number of data observations by number of attributes (predictors). In our case the required storage for the non-profit dataset was:

$$= 50,000 \text{ samples} * 306 \text{ attributes} =$$

$$= 15,300,000 \text{ bytes} = 15,300 \text{ Kbytes}.$$

The required storage space for the incremental linear regression is the size of the $X'X$ and the $X'Y$ matrices. In our case the required storage for the non-profit dataset was:

size of $X'X$ + size of $X'Y$ =

= (number of samples+1) * (number of variables) + (number of samples+1) * 1 =

= 50,001 samples * 306 attributes + 50,001 samples * 1 =

= 15,350,307 bytes ≈ 15,300 Kbytes

The required storage for the

In the case of the incremental cube-based linear regression model we save only the cubes in which there are data samples. For each one of those cubes we save the cube's number (which implies its location) and the number of data points inside this cube. Assuming we need only 1 byte to store the cubes location and another byte to store the number of data points in the cube, the actual amount of storage requirements to represent the data in the cube-based approach, is:

Number of cubes that actually contain data * (memory needed to store the cubes location + memory needed to store the number of data point in this cube) =

= 2* Number of cubes that actually contain data

The required storage for the non-profit dataset depend on the chosen size of the cubes, the results for different number of cubes (based on different cubes sizes) are summarized in the following table:

Original linear regression	Incremental Linear Regression	"Cube-based" incremental linear regression	
Data set size (K bytes)	Matrix size (K bytes)	Number of "Cubes"	"Cubes" memory (K bytes)
15,300	15,350	41215	41
15,300	15,350	31208	31
15,300	15,350	27247	27

Table 12 : Storage usage comparison for linear regression algorithms

This table clearly shows that in any case the cube-based approach attains a significant reduction in storage requirements to run the data mining models.

7.7.4 CPU Usage Results

Assuming there are d dimensions, n samples.

The needed data in each case is:
- Original linear regression:
    - The product of X' and the X matrices: Both matrices are of size $n*d$. Multiplication of these matrices results in a matrix of size $d*d$. Thus, the number of operations to multiply these two matrices are: $(d*d)*(2*d)$ operations.
    - The product of X' and the Y matrices yield a matrix of size $1*d$. The number of operations required to multiply these matrices is $(1*d)*(2*d)$ operations
    - Multiplying (X'X) with (X'Y) yield a matrix with dimension $1*d$. The number of operations required is $(1*d)*(2*d)$.

Adding, the total number of operations =

$(d*d)*(2*d) + (1*d)*(2*d) + (1*d)*(2*d) =$

$d^2 *(2d+2+2) = d^2 *(2d+4) = 2d^3+4d^2$

- Incremental linear regression: :
    - Updating the $X'X$ matrix of size d*d. For each cell in the matrix we need to add a product of 2 numbers. Therefore the number of operations required for this stage is d*d*2
    - Updating the $X'Y$ matrix of size dx1. For each cell in the matrix we need to add a product of 2 numbers. The required number of operations for this stage is $1*d*2$
    - Multiply a matrix of size d*d with a matrix of size dx1 matrix

123

requires for each cell n+1 multiplications and addition for a total of $d*(n+1)*2$ operations

Adding, the total number of operations = $d*d*2 + 1*d*2 + d*(n+1)*2 = 2d*(d+1+n+1) = 2d*(d+n+2) = 2d^2+2nd+4d$

- "Cube-based" model:
    - Finding the relevant cube – in the most pessimistic case, finding the model requires performing one operation (division) on each dimension. Therefore d operations are needed in this case.
    - Updating the cube – After the cube was found all is needed is to increment the number in this cube: 1 additional operation.
    - Re-calculating the model – in order to re-calculate the model, the matrices need to be created and multiplied. This step require as many operations as in the first case (simple linear regression), $d^2*(2d+4)$

Total needed operations = $2d^3+4d^2+d+1$

The results for different number of cubes are summarized in the following table:

	Original linear regression	Incremental linear regression	cube-based Linear regression
Needed operations	$2d^3+4d^2$	$2d^2+2nd+4d$	$2d^3+4d^2+d+1$

Table 13 : CPU usage for linear regression algorithms

This table shows that the incremental linear regression algorithm requires the fewest computational resources while the two other model requires similar resources.

7.8 Sensitivity Analysis for the Cubes Algorithm

7.8.1 The Effect of the Cube Size

The accuracy of the returned linear regression can be affected by several elements. The element that has the largest effect on the quality of the returned model is the size of the "cubes". When the cubes are larger, then a smaller number of cubes are needed and thus the memory requirement of the algorithm decreased. At the same time, the accuracy of the data (for the linear regression algorithm) is reduced the therefore, the accuracy of the returned model is reduced.

On the other hand, smaller "cubes" mean that more memory is required but the returned results are more accurate.

The size of the cubes and the number of cubes are dependent variables. When the size of the cube is decreased, a larger number of cubes are required, and vice-versa, larger cubes means fewer cubes are needed.

7.8.2 The Effect of Using Cubes

When using the cubes model, the actual data points are not used but the location of the cubes is used. This section analyzes the effect of using the cube's location (instead of the actual data point) on the returned linear regression.

The regression line is generally represented by the following equation [9]:

$$Y = X * B$$

where:

B is the coefficients vector,

Y is the predicted values vector,

X is the matrix of data points.

In order to find the regression coefficients the above equation is converted into

$$B = (X X)^{-1} X Y$$

To compare the actual data point results with the cube results we will define the following

Definition #1 - B_o is the result of using the original data point in the regression

$$B_o = (X'X)^{-1}X'Y$$

Definition #2 - ΔX_i represent the cube size for the ith dimension

Definition #3 - ΔX is the matrix representing the cubes sizes. The first column of the matrix is all 0s as there are no "cubes" defined on the constant, only on the problem's dimensions

$$\Delta X = \begin{pmatrix} 0 & \Delta X_1 \\ 0 & ... \\ 0 & \Delta X_n \end{pmatrix}$$

Where ΔX_i is the cube size for the ith dimension.

This matrix will allow us to convert the original data point representation into their cube representation, as we define $W = X + \Delta X$

Lemma #1 – $X_i \approx X_i + \Delta X_i$

Proof: As X_i represent the ith variable in the regression and ΔX_i represent the size of the cubes of the ith variable, we can clearly see that the effect of adding to cube size (or cube error) to the data is minimal. The values of X_i are significantly bigger then the values of ΔX_i and therefore the effect of the addition is minimal.

Definition #4 - B_c is the result of using the data cubes in the regression

$$B_c = \left[(X + \Delta X)'(X + \Delta X) \right]^{-1} (X + \Delta X)'Y$$

Instead of using the actual data points X , the values of X plus the error created using the cubes model was used. Therefore, X was replaced by $(X + \Delta X)$ where ΔX is the size of the cube.

Please note that this equation represents the values of B_c with maximal error as we are assuming an error size of ΔX for value in X .

<u>Theorem 1</u>
$B_o \approx B_c$.

Proof:

B_c can be expressed as a multiplication of 3 terms:

$$B_c = \left[(X + \Delta X)'(X + \Delta X) \right]^{-1} (X + \Delta X)' Y =$$
$$[X'X + X'\Delta X + \Delta X'X + \Delta X'\Delta X]^{-1}(X + \Delta X)'Y =$$

$$\underbrace{\hspace{6cm}}_{\text{Term 1}} \quad \underbrace{\hspace{2cm}}_{\text{Term 2}} \underbrace{\hspace{0.5cm}}_{\text{Term 3}}$$

The equivalent terms in B_o are:

$$B_o = \underbrace{(X'X)^{-1}}_{\text{Term 1}} \underbrace{X'}_{\text{Term 2}} \underbrace{Y}_{\text{Term 3}}$$

Based on that we can now proceed into analyzing each term in B_c and compare it the equivalent term in B_o:

I . We can easily see that the third term in both B_o and B_c is the same.

II. We second term of B_c is $X + \Delta X$ and for B_o it is X . Based on Lemma #1 described above these two terms are very similar (ΔX is relatively small in compared to X).

III. The first term of B_c is constructed from the sum of the 4 sub-terms: $X'X$, $X'\Delta X$, $\Delta X'X$ and $\Delta X'\Delta X$. Analyzing these terms we see that
- $X'X$ which is the same as the first term in B_o
- $X'\Delta X$ which is relatively small based on the assumption above (the X' matrix is multiplied in the ΔX which has very small values)
- $\Delta X'X$ which is relatively small based on the assumption above (the X matrix is multiplied in the $\Delta X'$ which has very small values)

- $\Delta X' \Delta X$ which is very small. As the size of the cube is relatively small we when we multiply it in itself we get very small values.

Therefore, values $X'X \approx X'X + X'\Delta X + \Delta X'X + \Delta X'\Delta X$ and furthermore, the values of $[X'X + X'\Delta X + \Delta X'X + \Delta X'\Delta X]^{-1} \approx (X'X)^{-1}$

As we have seen that the three terms in B_o and B_c are of similar values, we have proven that $B_o \approx B_c$.

The consequence of Theorem 1 is that the linear regression created from the original data is very similar to the liner regression created from the cubes data. In order to demonstrate these findings, a simple one variable sample will be used.

Assuming $X = \begin{pmatrix} 1 & 3 \\ 1 & 4 \\ 1 & 5 \end{pmatrix}$

Now, assume we use 10 segments dimension we get $\Delta X = \begin{pmatrix} 0 & 0.3 \\ 0 & 0.4 \\ 0 & 0.5 \end{pmatrix}$. The first column is 0 since there are no "cubes" defined on the constant, only on the problem's dimensions.

Under these assumptions we get

$$X' = \begin{pmatrix} 1 & 1 & 1 \\ 3 & 4 & 5 \end{pmatrix} \text{ and } \Delta X' = \begin{pmatrix} 0 & 0 & 0 \\ 0.3 & 0.4 & 0.5 \end{pmatrix}$$

The original $X'X = \begin{pmatrix} 1 & 12 \\ 12 & 50 \end{pmatrix}$

$$B_o = (X'X)^{-1} X'Y = \begin{pmatrix} -0.01 & 0.13 \\ 0.13 & -0.53 \end{pmatrix} \begin{pmatrix} 1 & 1 & 1 \\ 3 & 4 & 5 \end{pmatrix} Y = \begin{pmatrix} 0.1 & 0.09 & 0.07 \\ -0.15 & -0.02 & 0.11 \end{pmatrix} Y$$

128

When using the cubes, we get

$$X'\Delta X = \begin{pmatrix} 0 & 1.2 \\ 0 & 5 \end{pmatrix}$$

$$\Delta X'X = \begin{pmatrix} 0 & 0 \\ 1.2 & 5 \end{pmatrix}$$

$$\Delta X'\Delta X = \begin{pmatrix} 0 & 0 \\ 0 & 0.5 \end{pmatrix}$$

$$B_c = [X'X + X'\Delta X + \Delta X'X + \Delta X'\Delta X]^{-1}(X + \Delta X)'Y =$$
$$\begin{pmatrix} -0.01 & 0.12 \\ 0.12 & -0.53 \end{pmatrix} \begin{pmatrix} 1 & 1 & 1 \\ 3.3 & 4.4 & 5.5 \end{pmatrix} Y = \begin{pmatrix} 0.09 & 0.08 & 0.07 \\ -0.15 & -0.02 & 0.11 \end{pmatrix} Y$$

The resulted B_o and B_c are very similar, and therefore the use of the "cubes" has only minor (if any) effect on the received results. The returned model when using the cubes is as good as when using the non-incremental linear regression.

7.8.3 Results with Different Cubes Sizes
The cubes algorithm has been implemented on the DMEF "non-profit" dataset with different cubes sizes. The results were:

	Linear regression using the cubes	
Number of cubes	27247	31208
R^2	0.204	0.2022

Table 14 : Linear regression results with different cube sizes

These results show that the resulted model is of similar quality when the number of cube is changed. The reason for this result is that most of the variables in the data are binary, and therefore 2 "cubes" were created for each one of them. The only difference is the number of cubes occurred in the non-binary variables which were few, and therefore of minimal effect on the result.

This table can also be used to show the cube's ability to handle noise in the data (as described in the previous chapters). This table clearly shows that when the number of cubes increases, then smaller cubes is used which means that the cubes can "absorb" less noise, and then a less accurate (and more general) model is created.

7.9 Conclusions

This chapter described the incremental algorithm for regression using the cubes model. The main problem in creating an incremental version of the linear regression algorithm was finding a way in which all of the processed data were saved. The problem was solved using the cubes model. This model allows saving the approximate location of each new sample, and to still use a fixed amount memory.

Tests performed on the incremental regression algorithm showed that using the "cubes" (instead of the actual data sample) has only a minor effect on the quality of the produced model. In addition this algorithm fulfills all the requirements from incremental algorithm like: handling noise in the data, no effect on the order of the data, etc.

When the cubes are created based on the data characteristics and with the needed accuracy then the cubes hold an accurate representation of the range of the data in the problem space. In case that not all of the data characteristics are known in advance there may be cases in which the cubes will not be created in the optimal manner and hence will not represent the data samples accurately. In cases where the returned data has different characteristics than expected in advance it is recommended to reconstruct the cubes infrequently.

8 Logistic Regression

8.1 Introduction

Logistic regression is used in order to express the relationship between a discrete outcome (dependent variable) and a set of independent variables. In this work we focus on the simplest case where the outcome variable is binary Yes/No, such as purchase/no purchase in marketing applications. We develop an incremental logistic regression model, based on the cube-based data representation, and compare its results to those obtained based on the original dataset. Unlike in the linear regression case, no analytical incremental algorithm exist for logistic regression, perhaps leaving the incremental approach based on the multi dimensional cubes as the only means for incremental knowledge update.

8.2 The Logistic Regression Model

Two approaches have been devised to formulate binary choice problems, one is based on the relations between odds and probabilities, the other, which is more general, is based on the utility function approach of MacFadden [79]. We pursue the utility approach here.

To recall, in the linear regression case, the model is of the form:

$$Y_i = \beta' X_i + \varepsilon_i$$

Where:

Y_i - The continuous choice variable for observation i

X_i - Vector of explanatory variables, or predictors, for observation i

β - Vector of coefficients, estimated based on real observations.

ε_i - Random disturbance, or residual, of observation i, and there exist

$E(\varepsilon_i)=0$

In binary choice models, where the outcome variable assumes a value of 0 and 1, we assume that there is an underlying latent variable Y_i^* defined by the linear relationship:

$$Y_i^* = \beta' X_i + \varepsilon_i$$

Where Y_i^* is the "utility" that the customer derives by making the choice (e.g., purchasing a product). But in practice, Y_i^* is not observable. Instead, one observes the response variable Y_i, which is related to the latent variable Y_i^* by:

$$Y_i = \begin{cases} 1 & if \ Y_i^* > 0 \\ 0 & otherwise \end{cases}$$

From the two equations above, we obtain:

$$Prob(Y_i = 1) = Prob(Y_i^* = \beta' X_i + \varepsilon_i > 0)$$
$$= Prob(\varepsilon_i > -\beta' X_i) = 1 - F(-\beta' X_i)$$

Which yields, for symmetrical distribution of ε_i around zero:

$$Prob(Y_i = 1) = F(\beta' X_i)$$
$$Prob(Y_i = 0) = F(-\beta' X_i)$$

Where $F(\cdot)$ denotes the CDF of the disturbance ε_i.

The parameters $\beta's$ are estimated by maximizing the likelihood function:

$$l(\beta) = \prod_{i=1}^{n} \xi(x_i).$$

One can conceive of the observations Y_i 's as realizations from the Bernoulli distribution with a probability of success $\pi(x_i) = F(\beta' X_i)$ and failure $[1 - \pi(x_i)] = F(-\beta' X_i)$. Hence we obtain:

$$\xi(x_i) = \pi(x_i)^{y_i} [1 - \pi(x_i)]^{1-y_i}$$

To find the coefficient estimate, it is easier mathematically to work with the log of the likelihood function:

$$L(\beta) = \ln[l(\beta)] = \sum \{y_i \ln[\pi(x_i)] + (1 - y_i)\ln[1 - \pi(x_i)]\}$$

Differentiating the log likelihood function with respect to all β_i, and setting the resulting expression equal to zero, we obtain the likelihood equations, the solution of which is the coefficient estimates:

$$\sum_{i=1}^{n}[y_i - \pi(x_i)] = 0 \quad \text{and}$$

$$\sum_{i=1}^{n} x_{ij}[y_i - \pi(x_i)] = 0$$

For $j=1,2,\ldots,d$.

These expressions are nonlinear and are often in an iterative process using search methods, such as Newton-Raphson, and others.

The functional form of the likelihood equations and the estimation process depend on the distribution function F(.). In case the distribution of ε_i is logistic, we obtain the **logit** model with closed-form purchase probabilities [79]:

$$Prob(Y_i = 1) = \frac{1}{1 + exp(-\hat{\beta}'X)}$$

$$Prob(Y_i = 0) = \frac{1}{1 + exp(\hat{\beta}'X)}$$

Where $\hat{\beta}$, the MLE (Maximum likelihood estimate) of β.

An alternative assumption is that ε_i is normally distributed. The resulting model in this case is referred to as the **probit** model. This model is more complicated to estimate because the cumulative normal variable does not have a closed-form solution. But fortunately, the cumulative normal distribution and the logistic distribution are very close to each other. Consequently, the resulting probability estimates are similar. Thus, for all practical purposes, one can use the more convenient and more efficient logit model instead of the probit model.

8.3 Incremental Analytical Logistic Regression

We assume now that the initial dataset used to build the logistic regression model consists of n observations, and the incremental dataset consists of m observations.

The first n observations yield the likelihood equations, as above:

$$\sum_{i=1}^{n}[y_i - \pi(x_i)] = 0 \text{ and}$$

$$\sum_{i=1}^{n}x_{ij}[y_i - \pi(x_i)] = 0 \text{ For } j=1,2,...,d.$$

After adding the new m samples, the likelihood equations become:

$$\sum_{i=1}^{n+m}[y_i - \pi(x_i)] = 0 \text{ and}$$

$$\sum_{i=1}^{n+m}x_{ij}[y_i - \pi(x_i)] = 0 \text{ For } j=1,2,...,d.$$

The latter equations for $n+m$ samples can be converted to be:

$$\sum_{i=1}^{n}[y_i - \pi(x_i)] + \sum_{i=n+1}^{n+m}[y_i - \pi(x_i)] = 0$$

$$\sum_{i=1}^{n}x_{ij}[y_i - \pi(x_i)] + \sum_{i=n+1}^{n+m}x_{ij}[y_i - \pi(x_i)] = 0$$

One can not decompose these equations to those which correspond to the initial set of data and those which correspond to the incremental set of data. And as a result, the analytical incremental algorithm for logistic regression can not take any shortcuts to estimate the coefficients. Unlike the linear regression case, there is no easy way to save a few summary statistics from the first model in order to build the incremental model. Here it seems that there no escape but to solve the likelihood equations from scratch, based on all the $n+m$ observations.

The major disadvantage here is that one needs to save the entire data samples, including the incremental samples, in order to update knowledge. As the volume of data increases, this approach might be computationally prohibitive.

8.4 Cube-Based Incremental Logistic Regression

We overcome the limitation of the analytical incremental approach for logistic regression by means of our cube-based approach. This approach calls for storing the X matrix using the Z matrix and the converting the Z matrix to the W matrix, which is then used to build the logistic regression model.

The cube-based incremental algorithm for logistic regression proceeds as follows:
1. Initialization step
   a. Set the boundaries of the problem's space for both the dependent and independent variables. The number of dimensions in the problem's space is marked as d.
   b. Decide on the size of the cubes
2. Update the relevant cube
   c. Get new observation
   d. For each observation $(x_{1,n+1}, ..., x_{i,n+1}, ..., x_{d,n+1})$ where $x_{i,j}$ indicates the ith attribute in the jth observation.
      i. Find the cube to which this observation belongs.
      ii. If this cubes has already been used
         then increase the counter for this cube (the only data stored for each

cube is the number of data points which are residue inside the cube), else create this cube with counter=1

3. Update the regression

  e. Using the data in the cubes solve the following equations in an iterative process:

$$\sum_{i=1}^{n+m}[y_i - \pi(w_i)] = 0 \text{ and}$$

$$\sum_{i=1}^{n+m} w_{ij}[y_i - \pi(w_i)] = 0$$

  For $j=1,2,...,d$.

4. For each new data arrives, return to step 2.

8.5 Implementation on the Non Profit Dataset

We now apply the cube-based incremental approach for logistic regression on the non profit dataset and compare the results to the non incremental model.

8.5.1 Original Logistic Regression Results

To build the logistic regression model on the non-profit dataset, we first use GainSmart [78] to choose the set of influential predicators and then run the logistic regression algorithm described using these predictors.

The results of the logistic regression algorithm were:
- Training dataset
  - $R^2 = 0.11$
- Response per decile

Validation non-cumulative results by decile				
% Customers	% Response	Actual response rate %	% response / % customers	Predicted response rate %
10	24.3	65.87	2.4	65.15
10	14.9	40.34	1.5	40.88
10	12.6	34.23	1.3	35.23
10	11.5	31.07	1.1	31.47
10	9.5	25.63	0.9	27.25
10	7.5	20.30	0.7	22.79
10	6.8	18.47	0.7	19.42
10	5.5	14.96	0.6	15.74
10	4.4	11.88	0.4	11.84
10	3.0	8.23	0.3	8.15

Table 15 : Logistic regression validation results

- Gain Charts

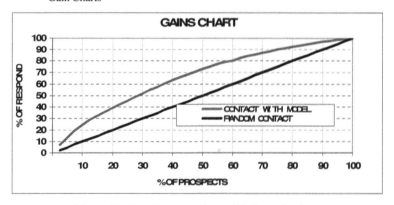

Figure 25 : Logistic regression validation gain chart

This is a pretty good model, with reasonable lift, no over-fitting and predicted results which are very close to the actual results.

8.5.2 Cube-Based Incremental Logistic Regression Results

As in the original (non incremental) case above, we have initiated the incremental logistic regression process by first applying GainSmart [78] to solve the feature selection problem. We then used the resulting predictors for in the incremental knowledge update. The data was divided into 3 portions: the first, 40,000 samples were used in order to create the original logistic regression model; the second 10,000 samples were used to incrementally update the model, and the third set of 50,000 samples used to validate the model results.

The results we obtained using the cube-based approach are:

- Training dataset
  - $R^2 = 0.17$
- Response per decile

Validation non-cumulative results by decile				
% Customers	% Response	Actual response rate %	% response / % customers	Predicted response rate %
10	31.2	61.37	3.1	64.65
10	20.3	39.90	2.0	37.30
10	13.4	26.31	1.3	24.49
10	9.8	19.17	1.0	17.82
10	6.7	13.15	0.7	14.42
10	4.8	9.35	0.5	11.90
10	3.5	6.98	0.4	10.23
10	4.7	9.33	0.5	8.70
10	3.2	6.33	0.3	6.42
10	2.4	4.72	0.2	4.56

Table 16 : Incremental logistic regression validation results

- Gain Charts

138

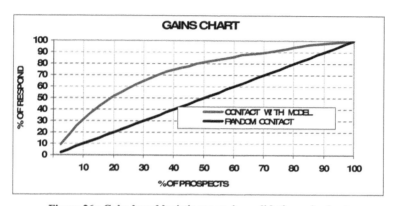

Figure 26 : Cube-based logistic regression validation gain chart

8.6 Results Analysis

We now compare the results of the cube-based incremental algorithm to those of the original model using several performance measures. The results are presented in Table 17:

	Original logistic regression	cube-based logistic regression
Validation R^2	0.11	0.17
Training K-S test	0.229	0.35
Validation K-S test	0.234	0.356
Gini Coefficient	0.223187	0.180263

Table 17 : Logistic regression results comparison

The following chart presents the gains charts of the two model one on top of the other.

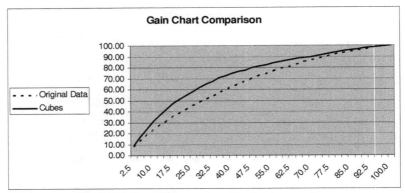

Figure 27 : Logistic regression gain chart comparison

The corresponding Lorenz Curves are exhibited in Figure 29.

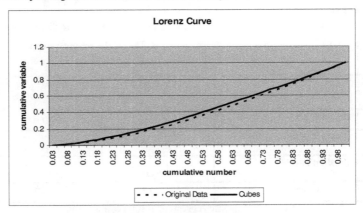

Figure 28 : Logistic regression Lorenz curves

Both the graphs and the tables above show some advantage of the cube-based model over the original logistic regression model. We envision that one source of the difference is because the incremental algorithm is better capable of handling noise in the data, and thus creates a better model. Perhaps these results are very specific to the dataset used in

140

this case, and not a general attribute of the cubes-based based approach. But at any case, the differences in the model results are not big and may not be statistically significant.

8.7 Conclusions

This chapter described the cube-based incremental algorithm for logistic regression. The analytical approach for incremental knowledge update doesn't seem to work for logistic regression, making the cube-based approach an attractive alternative. Comparing the model results obtained with the cube-based approach to the model results obtained with the original, non incremental, model, does not seem to show significant difference.

9 Classification

9.1 Introduction

Classification is a supervised learning method that allows assigning data samples to one of pre-defined classes. For example, in a banking application classifying new people applying for a loan as either "approved" or "not approved", in a direct marketing application, whether to classify a customer as a potential buyer or a potential non buyer.

Supervised classification models segment the dataset into decision trees based on observations with known class labels. Each terminal node in the tree (i.e., a node that is not split further) is then associated with one of the predefined classes, often based on economical considerations. For a marketing application, the classes would be a buyer and non buyer. The path leading from the root node to the terminal node represent the rule that assigns data points to that node.

Several algorithms have been proposed in the literature to create decision trees. In this work we deal with the CHAID (Chi-Square Automatic Interaction Detection) [19], which is the most commonly used decision trees algorithm. We start by describing the original CHAID algorithm, followed by the cube-based CHAID model. We then apply the non incremental and the incremental CHAID algorithms on the non profit dataset and compare the results.

9.2 The Original, Non Incremental, CHAID Classification Model

9.2.1 General Description

As with all decision trees, CHAID employs a systematic approach to grow a tree into "branches" and "leaves". In each stage, CHAID uses a chi-square test to find the "best" way to split a "father" node into several "children" nodes. In each stage of the tree creation process, some nodes are declared as "undetermined" and become the father nodes in the next stages of the tree development process, whereas some of the other are declared as "terminal" nodes. The process proceeds in this way until no more nodes are left in the tree which is worth splitting any further.

The process often starts with preprocessing to convert any continuous independent variables to categorical predictors using a binning process.

9.2.2 Calculating Chi-Square Statistics

The chi-square statistics for sample observations is given by the expression:

$$\text{Chi-square} = \sum \frac{(E-O)^2}{E},$$

Where:

O denotes the observed samples (processed samples) and

E the expected values.

The Chi-square test is used to test the hypothesis that the observed sample points come from a certain (pre-specified) distribution, say the normal distribution. CHAID uses the chi-square test to find the categories that are least significantly different with respect to the dependent variable (also called the test of independence)

For example, assuming we have the following observed values:

Observed	Sandals	Sneakers	Leather shoes	Boots	Other	Total
Male	6	17	13	9	5	50
Female	13	5	7	16	9	50
Total	19	22	20	25	14	100

Table 18 : Calculating chi-square statistics for a sample data

The expected value in each cell, under independence, is given by the product of marginal summation for the corresponding row and column divided by the total sum across all observations.

143

So, to derive the expected frequency of the males who prefer sandals (the upper most left cell), we multiply the corresponding row total (50) with the corresponding column total (19) and dividing the product by the total number of observations(100), i.e.,:

(50 * 19)/100 = 9.5.

Repeating these calculations for all cells, yield the following expected values matrix:

Expected	Sandals	Sneakers	Leather shoes	Boots	Other	Total
Male	9.5	11	10	12.5	7	50
Female	9.5	11	10	12.5	7	50
Total	19	22	20	25	14	100

Table 19 : The expected values table

Now, we can plug the expected values in the chi-square expression $\sum \frac{(E-O)^2}{E}$ and derive the Chi-square statistics.

For example, for the first cell we get: $\frac{(9.5-6)^2}{9.5} = 1.289$.

Summing these values over all cells yield the chi-square values, which is 14.026.

9.2.3 Formal CHAID Algorithm
The CHAID algorithm is:

Step 1: Prepare the data
  1. Categorize all continuous and nominal variables

Step 2: Choose the best predictor
  2. Use chi-square to find the best split criteria -
       For all candidate variable, that has not been already used by the algorithm, X_i with the categories $\{c_{i,1}, c_{i,2}, \ldots c_{i,n}\}$ do:

144

For all possible split of $\{c_{i,1}, c_{i,2}, \ldots c_{i,n}\}$ into m separate groups ($1 \le m \le n$), $\{\{c_{i,1}, \ldots, c_{i,t_1}\}, \{c_{i,t_1+1}, \ldots, c_{i,t_2}\}, \ldots, \{c_{i,t_m+1}, \ldots, c_{i,n}\}\}$ perform the following steps:

a. Create the observation matrix:

$$\begin{Bmatrix} o_{1,1} & \cdots & o_{1,n} \\ \cdots & & \cdots \\ o_{n,1} & \cdots & o_{n,n} \end{Bmatrix}$$

Where

Each rows in the matrix represent one of the groups in the split and the columns of the matrix represent different Y values.

$o_{p,q}$ is the number of samples from the relevant audience where p is one of the groups in the split (p=1,..,m) and q is one of the Y values. To better understand this, please see the example below.

b. Create the expected matrix

$$\begin{Bmatrix} e_{1,1} & \cdots & e_{1,n} \\ \cdots & & \cdots \\ e_{n,1} & \cdots & e_{n,n} \end{Bmatrix}$$

Where

$$e_{k,l} = \frac{\sum\limits_{i=1}^{n} o_{i,k} * \sum\limits_{i=1}^{n} o_{k,l}}{\sum\limits_{i=1}^{n}\sum\limits_{j=1}^{n} o_{i,j}}$$

c. For each possible split, calculate the chi-square values as follow:

$$\text{chi-square} = \sum_{i=1}^{n}\sum_{j=1}^{n} \frac{(e_{i,j} - o_{i,j})^2}{e_{i,j}}$$

Go over all the chi-square values and choose the one with the most significant p-value.

Step 3: Set the next node

3. Use the best split (found in the previous step) in order to split the audience for the node into sub-audiences

4. All insignificant different subsets are combined.

Step 4: Repeat the process

5. For each subset return to stage 2 until the data can no longer be split into statistically significant subsets.

In our case, the chi-square test is used to measure the difference between potential split of a predictor. Higher the chi-square value indicates that the difference between the groups is significant, implying a better split.

9.2.4 CHAID Sample

We demonstrate the CHAID algorithm for a simple dataset containing 2 independent variables X_1 and X_2 and one dependent variable Y, created randomly, as follows:

X1	X2	Y
1	2	1
2	0	1
2	1	2
2	1	2
1	2	0
0	1	1
2	2	1
1	2	2
1	1	1
0	2	2

Table 20 : CHAID sample data

Stage 1: Since all the variables are categorical, no additional preprocessing is required.

Stage 2: Checking all the possible splits for all variables.

Splitting X1 into 3 separate groups, the corresponding observed values table (with respect to Y) is:

For example, if X1 = 0, there are no observations with Y=0, one observation with Y=1 and another one observation with Y=2, yielding the row (0,1,1). And so on for all the other X1 values.

X1 / Y	0	1	2	Total
0	0	1	1	2
1	1	2	1	4
2	0	2	2	4
Total	1	5	4	10

Chi-square = 1.875

Splitting X1 into 2 separate groups, there are several ways for doing so:

X1 / Y	0	1	2	Total
0	0	1	1	2
1,2	1	4	3	8
Total	1	5	4	10

Chi-square = 0.3125

X1 / Y	0	1	2	Total
1	1	2	1	4
0,2	0	3	3	6
Total	1	5	4	10

Chi-square = 1.875

X1 / Y	0	1	2	Total
0,1	1	3	2	6
2	0	2	2	4
Total	1	5	4	10

Chi-square = 0.8333

Moving on to X2 and splitting it into separate groups, we get

X2 / Y	0	1	2	Total
0	0	1	0	1
1	0	2	2	4
2	1	2	2	5
Total	1	5	4	10

Chi-square = 2.1

And splitting X2 into 2 separate groups we get

X2 / Y	0	1	2	Total
0,1	0	3	2	5

2	1	2	2	5
Total	1	5	4	10

Chi-square = 1.2

X2 / Y	0	1	2	Total
0,2	1	3	2	6
1	0	2	2	4
Total	1	5	4	10

Chi-square = 0.8333

X2 / Y	0	1	2	Total
0	0	1	0	1
1	1	4	4	9
Total	1	5	4	10

Chi-square = 1.111

The highest chi-square value is associated with splitting X2 into 3 separate groups.

So the best way to split the root node is:

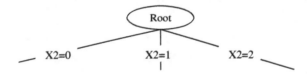

Figure 29 : CHAID sample - level 1

As a result of this step, the audience has been split into three mutually exclusive sub audiences. So we now repeat the process for each sub audience, noting that now we can only split sub audience according to X1.

For X2=0 there's only one observation with X1=2. Thus our observation table consists of only one row:

X1	X2	Y
2	0	1

The data in the second branch, X2=1, is

X1	X2	Y

148

0	1	1
1	1	1
2	1	2
2	1	2

The possible splits for this node are

X1 / Y	0	1	2	Total
0	0	1	0	1
1	0	1	0	1
2	0	0	2	2
Total	0	2	2	4

Chi-square=13.6

X1 / Y	0	1	2	Total
0	0	1	0	1
1,2	0	1	2	3
Total	0	2	2	4

Chi-square=6.9333

X1 / Y	0	1	2	Total
1	0	1	0	1
0,2	0	1	2	3
Total	0	2	2	4

Chi-square=6.9333

X1 / Y	0	1	2	Total
0,1	0	2	0	2
2	0	0	2	2
Total	0	2	2	4

Chi-square=13.6

Therefore, the best way to splits his node is either to 3 groups (0), (1),(2) or 2 groups (0,1) and (2), since both of them have the same largest chi-square value So we chose the second option . The sub audience represented by $X2 = (0,1)$ can not be split further, so this is a terminal node.

The data in the second branch, $X2=2$, is

X1	X2	Y
0	2	2
1	2	2
1	2	1
1	2	0
2	2	1

The possible splits for this node are

X1 / Y	0	1	2	Total
0	0	0	1	1
1	1	1	1	3
2	0	1	0	1
Total	1	2	2	5

Chi-square = 9.1667

X1 / Y	0	1	2	Total
0	0	0	1	1
1,2	1	2	1	4
Total	1	2	2	5

Chi-square = 6.25

X1 / Y	0	1	2	Total
1	1	1	1	3
0,2	0	1	1	2
Total	1	2	2	5

Chi-square = 4.1667

X1 / Y	0	1	2	Total
0,1	1	1	2	4
2	0	1	0	1
Total	1	2	2	5

Chi-square = 6.25

Clearly, the best way to split the sub audience for X2=2 is into the 3 groups corresponding to X1=0, X1=1 and X1=2, respectively.

None of the resulting sub audiences can be split any further, yielding the final tree:

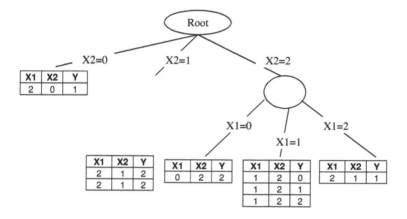

Figure 30 : CHAID sample - level 2

9.3 Classification Evaluation Criteria

In marketing applications, the objective of the tree classification process is to segment the audience into classes of likely buyers and likely non buyers. We therefore use marketing-oriented parameters to evaluate the classification results:

- Gains tables at the segment level, arranged by decreasing response rates of the segments. A "good" model will place the highly responsive segments at the top of the list and the least responsive segments at the bottom of the list. The larger the difference in response between the top responding segments and the least responding segments, the better the model. Gains charts also allow one to evaluate the quality of the model by comparing the results obtained for the training set to those for the validation set. If these results are more-or-less similar, this is an indication that the model is stable with no over fitting.
- Gini coefficients – as described above in the regression chapter.
- Receiver Operating Characteristic curve (ROC curve) – the ROC graph tracks the performance characteristics of the model, plotting the true positive rate against the

151

false positive rate for different possible cut points for defining "buyers" segments. An ROC curve demonstrates several things:

- It shows the tradeoff between sensitivity and specificity (any increase in sensitivity will be accompanied by a decrease in specificity).
- The closer the curve to the upper left corner, the better the model.
- And vice-versa, the closer the curve to the 45-degree diagonal of the ROC space, the worse the model.
- The greater the area under the graph, the better the model.

9.4 Incremental CHAID

The CHAID algorithm, which was described in the previous section, is a non-incremental algorithm. The algorithm uses all the samples in order to create the classification tree, so whenever new samples are added the classification tree needs to be re-calculated using all the former processed samples.

We discuss now an incremental CHAID algorithm for knowledge update, which is very similar to the original CHAID algorithm, except that we allow updating the chi-square values in light of new samples. We do this by saving the previous chi-square values, and then updating these values when new samples arrive, later the classification tree is updated accordingly. We discuss these steps in details below.

9.4.1 Incremental Chi-Square Update

Given two variables x_1 and x_2 each with several categories, we offer the following procedure to incrementally update the chi-square values when a new sample arrives.

1. Decrease from the chi-square the value $\sum \frac{(E-O)^2}{E}$ the cell which is affected by the new sample point.

2. Update the values corresponding to the new sample: the value of the observed cell, the row sum, the column sum and the observed value for this cell.

3. Update the chi-square statistics $\sum \frac{(E-O)^2}{E}$ accordingly.

To better understand the incremental update for the chi-square, a simple sample is shown.

Assume we have the following data table (observed values):

	Sandals	Sneakers	Leather shoes	Boots	Other	Total
Male observed	6	17	13	9	5	50
Female observed	13	5	7	16	9	50
Total	19	22	20	25	14	100

Table 21 : Incremental chi-square update - observed values

With the following expected values (as explained above):

	Sandals	Sneakers	Leather shoes	Boots	Other	Total
Male expected	9.5	11	10	12.5	7	50
Female expected	9.5	11	10	12.5	7	50
Total	19	22	20	25	14	100

Table 22 : Incremental chi-square update - expected values

The resulting chi-square value is 14.027

Now, assuming that the new observation is a male wearing leather shoes, then the observed data is:

	Sandals	Sneakers	Leather shoes	Boots	Other	Total
Male observed	6	17	14	9	5	51
Female observed	13	5	7	16	9	50
Total	19	22	21	25	14	101

Table 23 : Incremental chi-square update – updated observed values

(The changed values are marked)

And the expected values are:

	Sandals	Sneakers	Leather shoes	Boots	Other	Total
Male expected	9.5	11	10.604	12.5	7	51
Female expected	9.5	11	10	12.5	7	50
Total	19	22	21	25	14	101

Table 24 : Incremental chi-square update – updated expected values

(The changed values are marked)

To update the chi-square $\sum \frac{(E-O)^2}{E}$ all we need to do is decrease the old cell values and add the new value, i.e.,:

The new chi-square value = old chi-square value $- \frac{(10-13)^2}{10} + \frac{(10.604-14)^2}{10.604} =$

$14.027 - 0.9 + 1.087 = 14.214$

Thus, the update of the chi-square values is relatively simple and straightforward.

After updating the chi-square values, we need to update the classification tree, as described in the next section.

The update describe above showed that is it possible to incrementally update the Chi-Square value when new sample arrive. In case where multiple samples arrive, the update of the Chi-Square can be done in a similar way where all the effected cells in the observed and expected tables should be updated.

9.4.2 Incremental Classification Tree Update

To recall, in CHAID, each "father" node is split into its "children" nodes based on the chi-square test. Hence, when the new sample arrives, we need to check whether the split criteria are still correct. We do this for every node in the tree.

No change in the tree structure results, if the minimum p-values have not changed. But if the updated chi square value yields a smaller p-value than before, then we need to update the split of the affected node as well as subsequent the sub-tree.

In case where we update the tree for more then one data sample, we should just follow the same process for all effected nodes.

9.4.3 The Incremental CHAID Algorithm

The previous two sections described the analytical approach for incrementally updating a CHAID decision tree. The complete incremental analytical CHAID algorithm is:

Step 1: Chi-square update

1. Get the new sample(s)

2. Update the relevant chi-square values –for each variable that is affected:
   a. Subtract from the existing chi-square the value of $((E-O)^2/E)$ for the changed category.
   b. Update the observed values
   c. Update the expected values
   d. Add to the existing chi-square the new value of $((E-O)^2/E)$ for the changed category.

155

Step 2: Tree update

3. Review the tree from the top and down.

   For each node check that the split criteria for this node is correct (lowest significant p-value). If so, then no change in this node is required and the process can continue to the next node.

   Otherwise, if the split is to be changed, discard this node and the subsequent sub-tree, and re-construct the sub tree again using the correct splitting criteria.

4. Return to step #1.

Note that this algorithm has described a way to incrementally update a CHAID model in case of one new data sample, yet same logic applies in the case of processing multiple new data samples. In this case, there will be several changes in the observed and expected values, but the calculation of the chi-square will remain the same. Step #3 of the algorithm might require changing more nodes, but as all the whole tree is scans for correctness no change is needed there.

For this analysis one can easily see that "batching" data samples and processing them together will be much more efficient then processing the data samples one-by-one as they come. Since the algorithms review all the nodes in the tree, multiple changes can be done at once. This approach needs to be considered against the needed accuracy of the tree. As new samples arrive and the tree is not being updated with them its accuracy is effected.

While this algorithm allows updating a CHAID decision tree incrementally, it requires a relatively large amount of memory to save the required parameters. Also, the volume of computations is affected, as described below.

9.4.4 The Volume of Computation for the Incremental CHAID Algorithm

The incremental CHAID algorithm described above requires saving all the possible chi-square values and updating them whenever new samples arrive. In order to update the chi-square values the algorithm must have access to:

- The observed values
- The expected values
- The previous chi-square values.

Practically, this is a lot of information, which may render this approach prohibitive.

Two parameters that effect the number of possible splits: the variable's type and the number of categories for the variable.

The type of variable affects the way categorical variables can be grouped:

- In ordinal variables, only adjacent categories can be grouped together,
- A special case is an ordinal variable with a missing values which can be grouped with any other group
- In nominal variables, every two or more categories can be merged

Clearly, the larger the number of possible groupings for a variable, the larger the number of possible splits. The table below provides the number of possible splits for different number of categories and different variable types.

K	Ordinal	Ord + Missing	Nominal
2	1	1	1
3	2	3	3
4	3	5	7
5	4	7	15
6	5	9	31

7	6	11	63
8	7	13	127
9	8	15	255
10	9	17	511

Table 25 : Number of possible splits per variable type and values

For example, marital status is a nominal variable with four possible values (Single, Married, Divorced and Widow) can be split in 7 possible ways: (S,MDW), (M,SDW), (D,MSW), (W,SMD), (SM,DW), (MD,SD), (DW,SM).

And if we a database with 200 nominal attributes, each with 5 categories, the number of possible splits is 200*15=3000.

To further analyze this case, assuming that the response variable is binary, the algorithm will have to save 3000 observed matrices of size 5x2 (the number of the categories for the variable times the two binary options for the response variable), 3000 expected matrices of the same size, and 3000 calculated chi-square values. In total, the number of values to be saved is:

Observed + Expected + Chi-square values = 3000*5*2+3000*5*2+3000 =63,000 values

This is clearly a very large number of values for the algorithm to handle quickly and efficiently. In addition we need to keep in mind that often the number of possible categories for a variable exceeds 5.

This example shows that when dealing with large databases, the CHAID incremental algorithm may not be feasible because the number of values that need to be saved to allow for incrementally update knowledge may be too large to handle efficiently.

So, again, we resort to our cube-based approach to resolve this storage space issue.

9.5 The Cube-Based incremental CHAID

As mentioned several times in previous sections, the cube-based approach for knowledge update allows saving the processed data in a more "concentrated" way, thus requiring much less storage.

The cube-based incremental CHAID algorithm is as follows:

1. Initialization step
   a. Get the boundaries of the problem's space both for the dependent and independent variables. The number of dimensions in the problem's space is marked d.
   b. Decide on the size of the cubes.

2. Update the relevant cube
   c. Get new observations
   d. For each observation $(x_{1,n+1},...,x_{i,n+1},...,x_{d,n+1})$ where $x_{i,j}$ indicates the ith attribute in the jth observatio.
      i. Find the cube to which this observation belongs.
      ii. If this cubes has already been used

      then increase the counter for this cube (the only data stored for each cube is the number of data points which reside inside the cube),

      else create this cube with counter=1

3. Update the classification model
   a. Update the relevant chi-square values based the cube-based data representation.
   b. Go over the entire classification tree and update the nodes whose split was rendered not optimal, by the incremental data.

4. Repeat Step 2 for each new sample point.

Note that if the categories of the variables change as a result of the incremental data, one may have to modify the cube structure, as discussed in the pre-processing chapter.

9.6 Implementation on the Non-Profit Dataset

The DMEF "non-profit" dataset has been used in order to test the performance of the "cube-based" incremental CHAID algorithms described above and compare it to the results of the original CHAID algorithm.

The process of running the "cube-based" incremental CHAID algorithm contained three steps: First, the CHAID algorithm has been activated on the 40,000 training samples to create an initial CHAID model. Second, the "cube-based" incremental CHAID algorithm has been activated on additional 10,000 samples to incrementally improve the model. Third, the model created by the algorithm has been tested on a validation dataset that contained 50,000 samples.

The process of running the original CHAID algorithm contained only two steps: Running the algorithm on a training dataset of 50,000 samples and then validate the model on a validation dataset of 50,000 samples.

The training dataset in both cases contained the same samples and the validation dataset in both cases were also identical.

In both the CHAID algorithm and the "cube-based" incremental CHAID algorithm GainSmart [78] has been used in order to create the tree.

9.6.1 Original CHAID Results

The original CHAID algorithm created the following segments:

Response prob %	Customers	% Response	Actual Response	RR %	Actual % Customers	% Responses / RR %	Predicated profit	Actua profit
45.8	4960	10	2768	20.6	55.81	2.1	2838	57.21
36.44	4960	10	1867	13.9	37.64	1.4	1968	39.69
34.58	4960	10	1676	12.5	33.79	1.2	1730	34.88
31.08	4959	10	1578	11.7	31.82	1.2	1592	32.11
26.54	4960	10	1477	11	29.78	1.1	1435	28.94
23.33	4960	10	1181	8.8	23.81	0.9	1235	24.91
18.11	4959	10	981	7.3	19.78	0.7	1032	20.8
13.84	4960	10	786	5.8	15.85	0.6	807	16.28
11.86	4960	10	649	4.8	13.08	0.5	646	13.01
4.46	4959	10	477	3.5	9.62	0.4	445	8.98

Table 26 : Original CHAID results

160

The following graph is a gain chart of the original CHAID algorithm results.

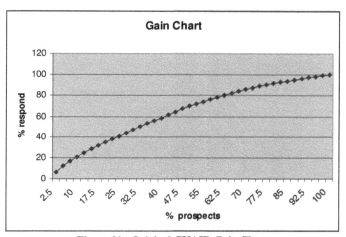

Figure 31 : Original CHAID Gain Chart

9.6.2 Incremental Cube-Based CHAID Results

The incremental "cube-based" CHAID algorithm was activated on the same dataset and yields the following results:

Response prob %	Customers	% Response	Actual Response	RR %	Actual % Customers	% Responses / RR %	Predicated profit	Actual profit
41.86	4960	10	2371	24.3	47.8	2.4	2489	50.18
32.78	4960	10	1881	19.3	37.92	1.9	1881	37.93
27.67	4960	10	1449	14.9	29.21	1.5	1509	30.42
21.03	4960	10	1093	11.2	22.04	1.1	1174	23.68
15.83	4960	10	971	10	19.58	1	926	18.68
11.94	4960	10	685	7	13.81	0.7	680	13.71
8.85	4960	10	473	4.9	9.54	0.5	531	10.71
7.52	4960	10	336	3.4	6.77	0.3	404	8.15
4.14	4960	10	307	3.1	6.19	0.3	269	5.42
1.45	4960	10	186	1.9	3.75	0.2	113	2.27

Table 27 : "Cube-based" CHAID results

The following graph describes the Gain chart of the "cube based" CHAID:

161

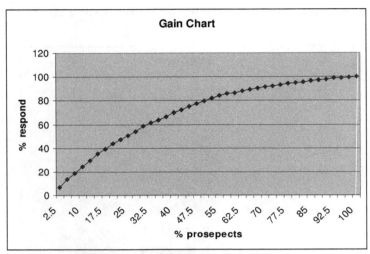

Figure 32 : Cube-based CHAID Gain Chart

9.7 Results Analysis

9.7.1 Comparing the Results

The goal of the tests described above was to check the similarity between the results received by the original CHAID algorithm and the "cube-based" CHAID algorithm. In order to test this we have compared the Gain charts, checked the similarity Gini coefficient comparison and run the Kolmogorov-Smirnov test on the received results.

Putting the 2 Gain results on the graph, yield the following results

162

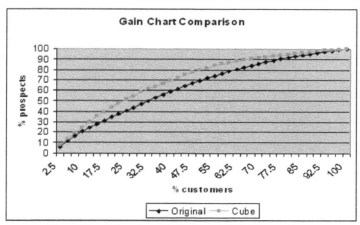

Figure 33 : Original and Cube-based CHAID gain charts

We can see that the results are very similar, and even the results of the cube based model are slightly better.

The results of the Gini coefficient tests were:

	Original CHAID	"cube-based" CHAID
Gini Coefficient	0.2425	0.2069

Table 28 : CHAID Gini coefficients

With the following Lorenz Curves:

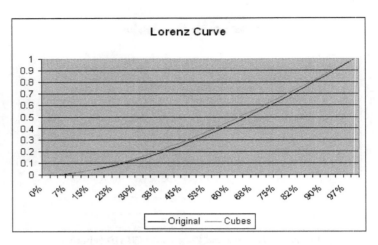

Figure 34 : CHAID Lorenz curves

The results of a Kolmogorov-Smirnov show that the maximum difference between the cumulative distributions, D, is: 0.21 with a corresponding P of: 0.764

Therefore, these two tests show that there is no significant difference between the results of the original CHAID algorithm and the results of the "cube-based" CHAID algorithm.

9.8 Conclusions

This chapter described the incremental "cube-based" classification algorithm. The main problem in creating an incremental version of the CHAID algorithm was finding a way in which all the processed data samples and addition internal information can be saved. The problem was solved using the cubes model. This model allows saving the approximate location of each new sample, and still uses a fixed amount memory.

Test performed on the "cube-based" incremental classification algorithm showed that using the "cubes" (instead of the actual data sample) has only a minor effect on the quality of the produced model. Therefore, the model produced from the incremental CHAID algorithm is as good as the model produced from the original CHAID algorithm.

10 Clustering

10.1 Introduction

The problem of grouping the data point into groups, or segments, which are homogenous within the group and heterogeneous between groups is known as clustering. Clustering is an unsupervised learning problem because the groups (classes) are not predefined as in the case of the classification model above.

In general, clustering algorithm can be divided into two groups: divisional algorithms and hierarchical algorithms. The divisional algorithms start from the entire audience as one group and split it further into smaller groups, for example the CLARANS [20] algorithm. The hierarchical algorithms start with the samples and merge them into groups, for example CURE [21].

Clustering algorithms create clusters with "similar" samples within clusters and "dissimilar" samples between clusters. In this work we use the K-Means algorithm, which is definitely one of the most well known algorithms for clustering. The K-means algorithm is a divisional algorithm that searches for a partition of the data points into clusters that minimizes the sum of a predefined distance measure of the points in the cluster from the center of the cluster, often referred to as the centroid.

We discuss the K-means algorithm in this chapter and create an incremental version of this algorithm, based on the cube-based model.

10.2 The Original K-Means Algorithm

10.2.1 General Description

The K-means algorithm partitions a set of n samples into a set of k ($k<= n$) clusters to minimize sum of distances of the sample points from the centroids. The K-Means is an iterative algorithm, as follows:

1. Pre specify the number of clusters
2. Randomly set the location of the clusters' centroids in the problem's space
3. Assign each data points to its closest cluster based on a predefined distance measure
4. Update the location of each centroid to reflect the data assignment of the previous step.
5. Repeat step #3 as long the termination conditions has not been met.

10.2.2 Formal Description

The K-means algorithm can be formulated as mathematical problem P [81]:

Minimize $P(C,Q) = \sum_{l=1}^{k} \sum_{i=1}^{n} c_{i,l} d(X_i, Q_i)$

Subject to $\sum_{l=1}^{n} c_{i,l} = 1, \quad 1 \le i \le n$

$$c_{i,l} \in \{0,1\}, \quad 1 \le i \le n, 1 \le l \le k$$

Where:

- C is an n by k partition matrix indicating the relations between the data samples and the centroids. The C matrix indicates the cluster to which each data sample belongs.
- $Q = \{Q_1, \ldots, Q_k\}$ is the centroid matrix.
- $d(a,b)$ is the squared Euclidean distance between two objects.

The basic K-means algorithm to solve problem P is given as follows [81]:

1. Choose an initial Q^0 and solve $P(C, Q^0)$ to obtain C^0. set $t=0$.

2. Let $\hat{C} = C'$ and solve $P(\hat{C}, Q)$ to obtain Q^{t+1}. If $P(\hat{C}, Q') = P(\hat{C}, Q^{t+1})$, output $\hat{C}, Q'$ and stop; otherwise go to step #3.

3. Let $\hat{Q} = Q^{t+1}$ and solve $P(C, \hat{Q})$ to obtain C^{t+1}. If $P(C', \hat{Q}) = P(C^{t+1}, \hat{Q})$, output $C', \hat{Q}$ and stop; otherwise let t=t+1 and go to step 2.

The K-means algorithm is an iterative algorithm. It starts by randomly choosing the location of the centroids. Then the algorithm finds the data points closest to each centroid, and updates the location of the centroid accordingly. The process repeats itself until there is no change in the location of the centroids or in the points that belong to each centroid.

10.2.3 Sample

We use a simple example to explain the flow of the K-means algorithm:
Assume a 2-dimensional space with 4 observations, as in Table 29, that needs to be partitioned into 2 clusters:

	$X_{i,1}$	$X_{i,2}$
X_1	1	1
X_2	3	3
X_3	8	7
X_4	8	9

Table 29 : K-Means sample data

The process will be as follow:

1. Randomly create the clusters, say:

$Q^0 = \begin{pmatrix} 4 & 9 \\ 5 & 3 \end{pmatrix}$, i.e., the first centroid is at (4,5) and the second is at (9,3), as shown in the diagram below:

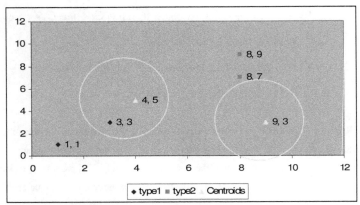

Figure 35 : K-means initial clusters

2. Calculate the distances for each data sample to each centroid :

	Distance to q_1	Distance to q_2
X_1	25	68
X_2	5	36
X_3	20	17
X_4	32	37

Therefore the W matrix will be

$$W^0 = \begin{pmatrix} 1 & 0 \\ 1 & 0 \\ 0 & 1 \\ 1 & 0 \end{pmatrix}$$, indicating that x_1, x_2, x_4 belong to cluster 1 and x_3 belong to cluster 2.

3. Based on the W^0, update the Q matrix so that each coordinate of the centroid is given by the average value of the corresponding variable across all data samples that belong to this cluster.

$$Q_1 = \begin{pmatrix} \dfrac{1+3+8}{3} & 8 \\ \dfrac{1+3+9}{3} & 7 \end{pmatrix} = \begin{pmatrix} 4 & 8 \\ 4.33 & 7 \end{pmatrix}, \text{ the first centroid is at (4,4.33) and the second}$$

is at (8,7).

4. The distances for these centroids are:

	Distance to q_1	Distance to q_2
X_1	20.111	45
X_2	2.778	17
X_3	23.111	16
X_4	37.778	20

And therefore the new W matrix will be

$$W^1 = \begin{pmatrix} 1 & 0 \\ 1 & 0 \\ 0 & 1 \\ 0 & 1 \end{pmatrix}, \text{ indicating that } x_1, x_2 \text{ belong to cluster 1 and } x_3, x_4 \text{ belong to cluster 2.}$$

5. Based on the W^1 the Q matrix will be updated to yield:

$$Q_1 = \begin{pmatrix} \dfrac{1+3}{2} & \dfrac{8+8}{2} \\ \dfrac{1+3}{2} & \dfrac{7+9}{2} \end{pmatrix} = \begin{pmatrix} 2 & 8 \\ 2 & 8 \end{pmatrix}, \text{ the first centroid is at (2,2) and the second is at}$$

(8,8), as shown in the following diagram.

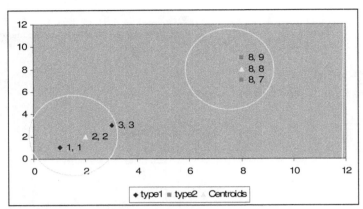

Figure 36 : K-means final clusters

After this step no additional changes yield any improvement, and thus terminating the algorithm.

10.3 Evolution Criteria of the Clustering Results

A good clustering algorithm will maximize the intra-cluster similarity while minimizing the inter-cluster similarity. This means that the objects inside each cluster are similar to each other, while they are different from objects in other groups.

We offer the following criteria to evaluate the quality of the clustering results:

- Maximum distance to centroid– the maximal distance between a data point and the centroid of the cluster to which it belongs
- Minimum distance to centroid – the minimal distance between a data point and the centroid of the cluster to which it belongs
- Mean distance to centroid – the mean value of the all the distances to the centroid
- Std. Dev. of distance to centroid – the STD of all the distances to the centroid
- Minimum Average distance – calculate the average distance for each cluster, and choose the minimum one.

170

- Maximum Average distance – calculate the average distance for each cluster, and choose the maximal value.
- Maximum distortion – the maximum value of distortion. Where the distortion is the sum of the square distances of all members from the centroid.
- Minimum distortion – the minimum value of distortion as described above.
- Average distortion – the average value of the distortion as described above.

10.4 The Incremental K-Means Algorithm

The K-means algorithm, which was described in the previous section, is a non-incremental algorithm, using all the samples in order to create the clusters.

The analytical incremental K-means algorithm operates in a similar way to the original K-means algorithm, as follows:
- Obtain new observation
- Find the cluster to which this observation belongs. This is the first centroid that needs to be changed.
- Update the location of the centroid to include the new data samples.
- Reallocate the observations that were affected by the above changes to their new clusters based on the distance measures.
- Calculate (update) the locations of the centroids.
- Repeat the process until no more changes to the clusters are feasible or worthwhile.

Formally, the algorithm proceeds as follows:
1. Start with the existing K centroids $Q=\{Q_1, \ldots, Q_k\}$
2. Read a new data sample
3. Find Q_i to which the new data sample is closest too, and update W accordingly and call it W^0.

4. Solve $P(C, Q^0)$ to obtain Q^0. set $t=0$.

5. Let $\hat{C} = C^t$ and solve $P(\hat{C}, Q)$ to obtain Q^{t+1}. If $P(\hat{C}, Q^t) = P(\hat{C}, Q^{t+1})$, output $\hat{C}$, Q^t and stop; otherwise continue.

6. Let $\hat{Q} = Q^{t+1}$ and solve $P(C, \hat{Q})$ to obtain C^{t+1}. If $P(C^t, \hat{Q}) = P(C^{t+1}, \hat{Q})$, output $W^t, \hat{Q}$ and stop; otherwise let $t=t+1$ and go return to step 5.

This algorithm requires all the existing (and already processed observations) will take part in the process of re-calculating the centroids. This requires saving all the observations, which renders the incremental K-Means algorithm in feasible.

10.5 The Cube-Based Incremental K-Means Algorithm

We present here a cube-based K-Means algorithm to update knowledge incrementally:

1. Initialization step
    a. Get the boundaries of the problem's space both for the dependent and independent variables. The number of dimensions in the problem's space is marked d.
    b. Decide on the size of the "cubes" (as described in the pre-processing section below).

2. Update the relevant cube
    c. Get a new observation $(x_{1,n+1}, ..., x_{i,n+1}, ..., x_{d,n+1})$ where $x_{i,j}$ indicates the ith attribute in the jth sample.
    d. Find the cube to which this observation belongs.
    e. If this cubes has already been used ,
       then increase the counter for this cube (the only data stored for each cube is the number of data points which are residue inside the cube),
       else create this cube with counter=1

172

3. Update the clusters

    f. Find Qi to which the observation is closest too,

    g. Update C matrix to include the observation. The new C matrix is called C^0.

    h. Solve $P(C, Q^0)$ to obtain Q^0. set t=0.

    i. Let $\hat{C} = C'$ and solve $P(\hat{C}, Q)$ to obtain Q^{t+1}.

    j. If $P(\hat{C}, Q^t) = P(\hat{C}, Q^{t+1})$,

        then output $\hat{C}$, Q^t and stop;

        otherwise continue.

    k. Let $\hat{Q} = Q^{t+1}$ and solve $P(C, \hat{Q})$ to obtain C^{t+1}.

    l. If $P(C', \hat{Q}) = P(C^{t+1}, \hat{Q})$,

        then output $C', \hat{Q}$ and stop;

        otherwise let t=t+1 and return to step j.

4. For each new data point, return to step 2.

To better understand this algorithm, a simple sample is described. We start off with the clustering matrix of the previous example:

	$V_{i,1}$	$V_{i,2}$	Type
X_1	1	1	1
X_2	3	3	1
X_3	8	7	2
X_4	8	9	2
Q_1	2	2	1
Q_2	8	8	2

Table 30 : Cube based K-means sample data

Now, assume a new sample is added in (1,5) of type 1.

The incremental process to update the centroids based on the new sample will be:

1. If there are existing centroids use them as a starting point and if not randomly create new centroids:

$Q^0 = \begin{pmatrix} 2 & 8 \\ 2 & 8 \end{pmatrix}$, the first centroid is at (2,2) and the second is at (8,8).

the following diagram describes this initial state

2. Calculate the distances for each data sample to each centroid and get:

	Distance to Q_1	Distance to Q_2
X_1	2	98
X_2	2	50
X_3	61	1
X_4	85	1
X_5	10	58

Therefore the W matrix will be

$W^0 = \begin{pmatrix} 1 & 0 \\ 1 & 0 \\ 0 & 1 \\ 0 & 1 \\ 1 & 0 \end{pmatrix}$, indicating that x_1, x_2 and x_5 belong to cluster 1 and x_3 and x_4 belong

to cluster 2.

3. Based on the resulting W^0 update the Q matrix, so that each centroid will be located at the average of all the data samples that belong to that centroid. Therefore,

$Q_1 = \begin{pmatrix} \dfrac{1+3+1}{3} & 8 \\ \dfrac{1+3+5}{3} & 7 \end{pmatrix} = \begin{pmatrix} 1.667 & 8 \\ 3 & 7 \end{pmatrix}$, the first centroid is at (1.667,3) and the

second is at (8,7).

After this step no additional changes are needed, so the algorithm terminates.

10.6 Implementation on a Realistic Dataset

To test the performance of the cube-based incremental K-means algorithm, we apply it on our Non Profit dataset. Unlike in the supervised learning models discussed above, the clustering process involves all predictors. Since the K-means algorithm is sensitive to the range of the variables, we have normalized all variables to the range 0-10, using the min-max transformation described in the preprocessing section.

10.6.1 K-Means Results for the Original Algorithm

The algorithm was activated with 100 clusters.

The detailed results are described in the appendix. The performance measures of the algorithm, discussed in 10.3, are described in the table below:

	Training dataset	Validation dataset
Number of Clusters	100	100
Maximum distance to centroid	1984	3331
Minimum distance to centroid	40	33
Mean distance to centroid	607.6	889.8
Std. Dev. of distance to centroid	169.8	171.1
Minimum Average distance	83.44	88.4
Maximum distortion	3936256	11095561
Minimum distortion	1600	1089

Table 31 : Original K-means results

10.6.2 The Cube-Based Incremental K-Means Algorithm Results

The cube-based K-Means incremental algorithm was also activated on the same Non-profit dataset, for comparison purposes.

The detailed clustering results are described in the appendix. The performance measures are summarized in Table 32:

175

	Training dataset	Validation dataset
Number of Clusters	100	100
Maximum distance to centroid	1952	3309
Minimum distance to centroid	75	83
Mean distance to centroid	626.8	945.9
Std. Dev. of distance to centroid	170.7	170.5
Minimum Average distance	159.2	165.1
Maximum distortion	3810304	10949481
Minimum distortion	5625	6889

Table 32 : Cube-based K-means results

10.7 Results Analysis

10.7.1 Results Comparison

The following table presents the performance measures of the original K-Means algorithm and the cube-based algorithm side-by-side:

	Original K-means algorithm	"cube-based" K-means algorithm
Number of Clusters	100	100
Maximum distance to centroid	3331	3309
Minimum distance to centroid	33	83
Mean distance to centroid	889.8	945.9
Std. Dev. of distance to centroid	171.1	170.5
Minimum Average distance	88.4	165.1
Maximum distortion	11095561	10949481
Minimum distortion	1089	6889

Table 33 : Clustering validation results comparison

These results show that the incremental cube-based algorithm yields results which are comparable to those of the original K-means algorithm

10.7.2 The Advantages of the Incremental Algorithm

In the original algorithm, all the observations are processed simultaneously; in the cube-based incremental approach, observations were processed one at a time, one-by-one. This may create situations in which the resulting clusters will be different from those obtained by processing all observations at once. We show this mathematically in this section:

Assume:

- There are at least two clusters

$$Q_i = (q_{1,i}...q_{d,i})$$
$$Q_j = (q_{1,j}...q_{d,j})$$

- The data set contains at least 4 data points

$$x_l = (x_{1,l}...q_{d,l}) \qquad where \qquad l = 1,2,3,4$$

  that comply to the following:

  - For a given dimension m the above data points fulfill

    $$x_{1,m} < x_{2,m} < x_{3,m} < x_{4,m}$$

  - $x_{2,m}$ is closer to $x_{1,m}$ then to $x_{3,m}$ i.e. $x_{2,m} - x_{1,m} < x_{3,m} - x_{2,m}$

  - $x_{3,m}$ is closer to the average of $x_{2,m}$ and $x_{1,m}$ then to $x_{4,m}$

    i.e. $x_{3,m} - \dfrac{x_{1,m} + x_{2,m}}{2} < x_{4,m} - x_{3,m}$

  - The data samples appear in the data set in the following order :

    $$...,x_1,...,x_4,...x_2,...,x_3,...$$

- In the original "k-means" algorithm:

  x_1 and x_2 were in cluster q_i and

  x_3 and x_4 were in cluster q_j

- In the incremental algorithm, q_i and q_j were not assigned yet, or

  q_i is located at (or near) x_1 and q_j is located at (or near) x_4

When the incremental algorithm processes these samples the results are:

- x_1 is processed by assigning it to q_i, and the location of the q_i is updated accordingly.
- x_4 is processed by assigning it to q_j, and the location of the q_j is updated accordingly.
- x_2 is processed and since it is closer to x_1 then it is assigned to q_i, the location of q_i is updated to be the average of
- x_3 is processed and since it is closer to the average of x_1 and x_2, then to x_4, then x_3 is assigned to q_i

The results from this incremental processing indicate that cluster q_i contains the points $\{x_1, x_2, x_3\}$ and the cluster q_j contain the point $\{x_4\}$. Therefore the resulting clusters are different than those obtained by the original algorithm.

In addition, when comparing the cumulative distances (over the m dimension) we get:
The original clustering algorithm =
$$\left(q_{i,m} - x_{1,m}\right)^2 + \left(q_{i,m} - x_{2,m}\right)^2 + \left(q_{j,m} - x_{3,m}\right)^2 + \left(q_{j,m} - x_{4,m}\right)^2$$
And for the incremental clustering algorithm =
$$\left(q_{i,m} - x_{1,m}\right)^2 + \left(q_{i,m} - x_{2,m}\right)^2 + \left(q_{i,m} - x_{3,m}\right)^2 + \left(q_{j,m} - x_{4,m}\right)^2$$

When eliminating the identical elements from both equations we get:
The original clustering algorithm = $\left(q_{j,m} - x_{3,m}\right)^2$
The incremental clustering algorithm = $\left(q_{i,m} - x_{3,m}\right)^2$

Since q_j is located at (or near) x_4 and q_i is located at $\dfrac{x_{1,m} + x_{2,m}}{2}$ then the distances are:

The original clustering algorithm = $\left(x_4 - x_{3,m}\right)^2$

The incremental clustering algorithm = $\left(\dfrac{x_{1,m} + x_{2,m}}{2} - x_{3,m}\right)^2$

And according to the assumptions described above ($x_{3,m} - \frac{x_{1,m}+x_{2,m}}{2} < x_{4,m} - x_{3,m}$), the distance for the incremental clustering algorithm is smaller then the distance for the original clustering algorithm.

This section has shown that given some simple pre-conditions, the clusters created by the incremental algorithm may be better than the clusters created by the original clustering algorithms. These conditions are simple and very likely to occur in practice, especially in large databases.

We use a simple example to demonstrate this phenomenon

Assume the following one-dimensional data points: 9, 1, 7, 3, 6, 5.5, 4.75 to be clustered into 2 clusters.
In the non-incremental case, the first cluster contains the points {9, 7, 6, 5.5} and its centroid is at 6.875, while the second cluster contains the points {1, 3, 4.75} and its centroid is at 2.92.
In the incremental case, the whole process is described in the following table:

Sample num	Sample value	Cluster #1	Centroid #1	Cluster #2	Centroid #2
1	9	{9}	9	-	-
2	1	{9}	9	{1}	1
3	7	{9,7}	8	{1}	1
4	3	{9,7}	8	{1,3}	2
5	6	{9,7,6}	7.33	{1,3}	2
6	5.5	{9,7,6,5.5}	6.875	{1,3}	2
7	4.75	{9,7,6,5.5,4.75}	6.45	{1,3}	2

Table 34 : Incremental clustering sample results

Even though the starting points for both clusters were the same, the incremental and the original process yield different clusters. Also, the quality of the resulting clusters is different, with the total distance in the non-incremental case being 14.23 and in the

179

incremental case being 12.8. Consequently, the incremental algorithm yields better clusters than the non-incremental algorithm.

10.8 Z-Based K-Means Clustering

This section shows how the K-means algorithm can be modified to use the Z matrix instead of the W matrix (as defined in chapter 4).

Using the Z matrix instead of the W matrix results in significant savings in the amount of computations for the cube-based K-Means algorithm. Yet, this process is quite simple and straightforward.

In order to use the Z matrix instead of the actual observations, steps #3 and #4 of the K-Means algorithm (see Section 10.2.1) need to be changed.. All the other steps in the algorithm remain the same as they are not data related.

Step #3 of the K-means algorithm requires that we find the closest centroid to each of the data point. In order to use the Z matrix, we need to calculate the distance between two cubes, one is the data cube and the other is the centroid cube.

Given two cubes q and c, we define the distance between these two cubes as:

$$Distance = \sum_{i=1}^{d} \left[\left(\left\lfloor \frac{q}{k^{d-i}} \right\rfloor \bmod k \right) - \left(\left\lfloor \frac{c}{k^{d-i}} \right\rfloor \bmod k \right) \right]^2$$

Where:

d is the number of dimensions

k is the number of segments in each dimension (for simplicity we have assumed the same number for each dimension)

c is the cube number

For example, in a three-dimensional problem (d=3) where k=10, the distance between the cube 345 and cube number 149 is:

Distance =

$$\left[\left(\left\lfloor\frac{345}{10^2}\right\rfloor \bmod 10\right)-\left(\left\lfloor\frac{149}{10^2}\right\rfloor \bmod 10\right)\right]^2+\left[\left(\left\lfloor\frac{345}{10^1}\right\rfloor \bmod 10\right)-\left(\left\lfloor\frac{149}{10^1}\right\rfloor \bmod 10\right)\right]^2+\left[\left(\left\lfloor\frac{345}{10^0}\right\rfloor \bmod 10^0\right)-\left(\left\lfloor\frac{149}{10^0}\right\rfloor \bmod 10^0\right)\right]^2=$$

$$[(3)-(1)]^2+[(4)-(4)]^2+[(5)-(9)]^2=20$$

Step #4 of the K-means algorithm requires that we find the average location of a set of data cubes. Given a set of n cubes $(c_1, c_2, \ldots, c_n)$ the average locations of these cubes is:

$$\text{Average cube location} = \sum_{j=1}^{d}\left[\frac{\frac{1}{n}\sum_{i=1}^{d}\left\lfloor\left\lfloor\frac{c_i}{k^{d-i}}\right\rfloor \bmod k\right\rfloor}{cube\_size_j} * k^{d-j}\right]$$

Where

d is the number of dimensions

n is the number of cubes

k is the number of segments in each dimension (for simplicity we have assumed the same number for each dimension)

$max\ w_i$ is the maximum value on the ith dimension

$min\ w_i$ is the minimum value on the ith dimension

and

$cube\_size_i=(max\ x_i - max\ x_i)\ /\ k$

For example, in a three-dimensional space (d=3) where k=10, and the average location of cubes 123 and 456 is:

Assuming that the min value for all dimensions is 0 and the max is 10.

Average cube location =

$$\left[\frac{\frac{1}{2}\sum_{i=1}^{d}\left\lfloor\left\lfloor\frac{c_i}{k^{d-i}}\right\rfloor \bmod 10\right\rfloor}{1}*10^2\right]+\left[\frac{\frac{1}{2}\sum_{i=1}^{d}\left\lfloor\left\lfloor\frac{c_i}{k^{d-i}}\right\rfloor \bmod 10\right\rfloor}{1}*10^1\right]+\left[\frac{\frac{1}{2}\sum_{i=1}^{d}\left\lfloor\left\lfloor\frac{c_i}{k^{d-i}}\right\rfloor \bmod 10\right\rfloor}{1}*10^0=\right]$$

$$\left[\frac{\frac{1}{2}[1+4]}{1}\right]*10^2+\left[\frac{\frac{1}{2}[2+5]}{1}\right]*10^1+\left[\frac{\frac{1}{2}[3+6]}{1}\right]*10^0=234$$

The fact that steps#3 and #4 of the K-Means algorithm can be executed on the Z matrix implies that one does not need either the X or the W matrix to incrementally cluster the data.

To further demonstrate this, we use a small example:

Assume that the following 2 dimensional data needs to be split up into 2 clusters

$w_{i,1}$	$w_{i,2}$
1	1
3	3
8	7
8	9

Table 35 : Z-Based K-Means sample data

In this case the X matrix is:

$$X=\begin{pmatrix}1&1\\3&3\\8&7\\8&9\end{pmatrix}$$

Assuming 10 segments for each dimension, the Z matrix is: $Z=\begin{pmatrix}11&33&87&89\\1&1&1&1\end{pmatrix}$

Note: In this case there are no binary attributes so the second row of the Z matrix has been eliminated.

The K-means process will then be:

182

1. Randomly place the centroids, say one centroid at cube 45 and the other at cube 93, as described in the diagram below:

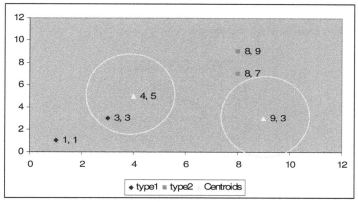

Figure 37 : Z-Based K-means initial clusters

2. Calculate the distances for each data sample to each centroid:

Distance between c_1 (cube 45) and q_1 (cube 11) =

$$= \sum_{i=1}^{d} \left[x_i - \left(\left\lfloor \frac{c_i}{k^{d-i}} \right\rfloor \mod k \right) \right] =$$

$$= \left[\left(\left\lfloor \frac{45}{10^{2-1}} \right\rfloor \mod 10 \right) - \left(\left\lfloor \frac{11}{10^{2-1}} \right\rfloor \mod 10 \right) \right]^2 + \left[\left(\left\lfloor \frac{45}{10^{2-2}} \right\rfloor \mod 10 \right) - \left(\left\lfloor \frac{11}{10^{2-2}} \right\rfloor \mod 10 \right) \right]^2 =$$

$$= [4-1]^2 + [5-1]^2 = 25$$

Distance between c_1 (cube 93) and q_2 (cube 11) =

$$\sum_{i=1}^{d} \left[x_i - \left(\left\lfloor \frac{c_i}{k^{d-i}} \right\rfloor \mod k \right) \right] =$$

$$= \left[\left(\left\lfloor \frac{93}{10^{2-1}} \right\rfloor \mod 10 \right) - \left(\left\lfloor \frac{11}{10^{2-1}} \right\rfloor \mod 10 \right) \right]^2 + \left[\left(\left\lfloor \frac{93}{10^{2-2}} \right\rfloor \mod 10 \right) - \left(\left\lfloor \frac{11}{10^{2-2}} \right\rfloor \mod 10 \right) \right]^2 =$$

$$= [9-1]^2 + [3-1]^2 = 29$$

Etc.

The results for all the distances are:

	Distance to q_1	Distance to q_2
c_1	25	68
c_2	5	36
c_3	20	17
c_4	32	37

Based on these results, c_1,c_2,c_4 are assigned to cluster 1 and c_3 to luster 2. After this assignment, the location of each centroid is updated to be:

First centroid location (q_1)= average location for c_1,c_2 and c_4 =

$$\left[\frac{\frac{1}{3}\sum_{i=1}^{d}\left\lfloor \left\lfloor \frac{c_i}{k^{d-i}} \right\rfloor \bmod 10 \right\rfloor}{1} \right]*10^1 + \left[\frac{\frac{1}{3}\sum_{i=1}^{d}\left\lfloor \left\lfloor \frac{c_i}{k^{d-i}} \right\rfloor \bmod 10 \right\rfloor}{1} \right]*10^0 =$$

$$\left[\frac{\frac{1}{3}[1+3+8]}{1} \right]*10^1 + \left[\frac{\frac{1}{3}[1+3+9]}{1} \right]*10^0 =$$

44

Second centroid location (q_2) = average location for c_3 = 87

3. The updated distances for these centroids are:

	Distance to q_1	Distance to q_2
c_1	**18**	85
c_2	**2**	41
c_3	25	**0**
c_4	41	**4**

And therefore, c_1 and c_2 are assigned to the first cluster while c_3 and c_4 to the second cluster.

Based on that assignment, the new centroid locations are:

First centroid location (q_1)= average location for c_1 and c_2 =

$$\left[\frac{\left| \frac{1}{2} \sum_{i=1}^{d} \left\lfloor \frac{c_i}{k^{d-i}} \right\rfloor \bmod 10 \right|}{1} \right] * 10^1 + \left[\frac{\left| \frac{1}{2} \sum_{i=1}^{d} \left\lfloor \frac{c_i}{k^{d-i}} \right\rfloor \bmod 10 \right|}{1} \right] * 10^0 =$$

$$\left[\frac{\left| \frac{1}{2}[1+3] \right|}{1} \right] * 10^1 + \left[\frac{\left| \frac{1}{2}[1+3] \right|}{1} \right] * 10^0 =$$

22

Second centroid location (q_2)= average location for c_3 and c_4 =

$$\left[\frac{\left| \frac{1}{2} \sum_{i=1}^{d} \left\lfloor \frac{c_i}{k^{d-i}} \right\rfloor \bmod 10 \right|}{1} \right] * 10^1 + \left[\frac{\left| \frac{1}{2} \sum_{i=1}^{d} \left\lfloor \frac{c_i}{k^{d-i}} \right\rfloor \bmod 10 \right|}{1} \right] * 10^0 =$$

$$\left[\frac{\frac{1}{2}[8+8]}{1} \right] * 10^1 + \left[\frac{\frac{1}{2}[7+9]}{1} \right] * 10^0 =$$

88

The following diagram shows these final centroids location.

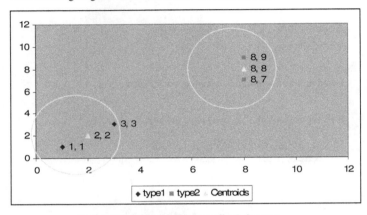

Figure 38 : Z-based K-means final clusters

No additional changes are required beyond this step.

This example shows that the K-means incremental algorithm can be implemented directly on the Z matrix, yielding results which are identical to those based on the W matrix. Because the Z matrix is much smaller than the W matrix, one can save a lot of computations.

10.9 Sensitivity Analysis of the Cube-Based Algorithm

In this section we analyze the sensitivity of the resulting clusters as a result of using the cube-based approach.

10.9.1 Analyzing the Effect of Using the Cubes

To recall, the centroid of a cluster is calculated as the average of the data points in the cluster.

Using the actual data point, the location of the centroid $(q_1, ..., q_d)$ is

$$q_i = \frac{\sum_{j=1}^{m} x_j}{m}$$

While when using the cubes the location of the centroid is

$$q_i^{'} = \frac{\sum_{j=1}^{m}(x_j + \Delta x_j)}{m}$$

Where Δx_j is the error due to using the cubes and not the actual observations (which is half the size of the cube). Expanding the latter equation, we get:

$$q_i^{'} = \frac{\sum_{j=1}^{m}(x_j + \Delta x_j)}{m} = \frac{\sum_{j=1}^{m} x_j}{m} + \frac{\sum_{j=1}^{m} \Delta x_j}{m} = q_i + \frac{\sum_{j=1}^{m} \Delta x_j}{m}$$

This equation shows that the difference between q_i and $q_i^{'}$ is small and they are very similar to each other.

To show this similarity further we assume that all the cubes (over all the dimensions) are of equal size. Then expanding the above equation to be:

$$q_i^{'} = q_i + \frac{\sum_{j=1}^{m} \Delta x_j}{m} = q_i + \frac{m * \Delta x_j}{m} = q_i + \Delta x_j$$

Since Δx_j is small, the resulting q_i and $q_i^{'}$ are almost identical. Therefore using the cubes and not the actual data have only minor effect (is any) on the clustering results.

10.10 Conclusions

This chapter described the cube-based K-Means incremental clustering algorithm. Unlike all previous models, we showed here that the K-Means algorithm can work directly on the Z matrix, which, because the dimension of the Z matrix is much smaller than the dimension of the W matrix, results in significant savings in the volume of computations. Furthermore, the incremental clustering algorithm may yield better results than the original K-means algorithm, and that using the cubes instead of the actual data sample has only a minor effect on the quality of the resulting clusters (if any).

11 Rule Induction

11.1 Introduction

Rule induction algorithms interrogate the data base to finds relationships, called rules, between the data elements, of the form "If <antecedent> then <consequent>". For example, in a marketing application, finding find set of items which are bought together based on previous purchases.

One of the most popular methods for rule induction is the Apriori algorithm [27]. This approach consists of two steps: first, finding frequent itemset in the dataset, and second, creating rules from these itemsets.

We describe the Apriori algorithm in this chapter and offer an incremental version for it using the cube-based approach. The algorithm is activated on the non-profit dataset, comparing the results to those obtained with the non-incremental Apriori algorithm.

11.2 The Original Apriori Algorithm

The Apriori algorithm was introduced by Agrawal and Srikant [82]. To describe the algorithm, we introduce a few definitions first:

Let $I = \{i_1, i_2, ..., i_m\}$ be a set of m distinct items. A database transaction T is a set of items in I. A database D is a set of transactions. For example, I can represent products available in a supermarket (SKU's), a transaction T is the product purchased by a single buyer and D is the set of all the transactions.

A set of items is called an itemset. The number of items in an itemset is called the length of an itemset.

A transaction T is said to *support* an itemset $X \subseteq I$ if and only if it contains all items of X, i.e. $X \subseteq T$. The fraction of the transactions in D that support X is called the support of X, denoted as *Support(X)*. An itemset is considered frequent if and only if its support exceeds a minimum support threshold defined by the User.

For example: assume that $I=\{1,2,3,4,5\}$ with the minimum support of 0.75 and four database transactions:

1	$\{1,2,3,4,5\}$
2	$\{1,3\}$
3	$\{1,2\}$
4	$\{1,2,3,4\}$

Table 36 : Rule induction sample data

Then the frequent itemset are: $\{1\},\{2\},\{3\},\{1,2\},\{1,3\}$. For instance, itemset $\{1,2\}$ is frequent since three out of four transactions (transactions 1,3 and 4) contain items 1 and 2, i.e. the support of $\{1,2\}$ is 0.75.

In the Apriori algorithm we use the notation L_K to denote a frequent itemset of length k, and C_k to denote a "candidate" itemset – an itemset whose frequency needs to be checked in order to decide if it is a frequent itemset.

11.2.1 General Description

The Apriori algorithm is based on two steps: First, finding all the common itemsets in the database, and second creating rules from these itemset.

The first part of the Apriori algorithm works as follow:

1. $k = 1$
2. Frequent itemset generation - Go over C_k (the set of all candidate itemsets) and add each itemset whose support is larger than the minimum support to L_k (the set of all frequent itemsets)
3. Candidate itemset generation - Form C_{k+1} from L_k
4. $k = k+1$

5. Repeat 2-4 until C_k is empty

The second part of the Apriori algorithm creates association rules, based on the frequent itemsets, which meet predefined confidence and support levels.

11.2.2 The Formal Apriori Algorithm

The Apriori algorithm works as follow:

1. k=1
2. $C_k = \bigcup_{i \in I} \{i\}$
3. Create the first L_k
   - Initialize L_k as an empty set
   - For all $c \in C_{k+1}$
   - if support(c) > MinSupport
     then $L_k = L_k \cup \{c\}$
4. while L_k is not empty and k is smaller them k_{max} do:
   - Create C_{k+1} based on L_k
     1. for each $l1, l2 \in L_k$
        with $l1 = \{i_1, ..., i_{k-1}, i_k\}$
        and $l2 = \{i_1, ..., i_{k-1}, i_k'\}$
        and $i_k < i_k'$ do
           $l = l1 \cup l2 = \{i_1, ..., i_{k-1}, i_k, i_k'\}$
           if $\forall i \in l : l - \{i\} \in L_k$
           then $C_{k+1} = C_{k+1} \cup \{f\}$
   - Form L_{k+1} by pruning C_{k+1}
     1. For all $c \in C_{k+1}$ do s(c) = 0

2. For all $t \in T$ (all the transactions) do

   For all $c \in C_{k+1}$ do

   if $c \in t$ then s(c)=s(c)+1

3. Initialize L_{k+1} as an empty set

4. For all $c \in C_{k+1}$ do

   if s(c) $\geq s_{min}$

   then $L_{k+1} = L_{k+1} \cup \{c\}$

   o k=k+1

5. Generate association rules

   o For every non-empty subset A of X

   o Let C = X - A.

   o A $\Rightarrow$ C is an association rule if,

      confidence(A $\Rightarrow$ C) $\geq$ minConfidence

11.2.3 Apriori Algorithm Example

To further explain this algorithm, a simple example is analyzed. Given the following data

Item set
1,3,4
2,3,5
1,2,3,5
2,5

Table 37 : Apriori sample data

Assuming that the required minimum support is 0.5, we create the association rules as follows:

Scan the data set to create C_1, L_1 and C_2

$C_1 = \{1\},\{2\},\{3\},\{4\},\{5\}$ with support 2, 3, 3, 1 and 3, respectively.

The support of itemset $\{4\}$ is only 0.25 (1 out of 4 data samples) which is less than the required MinSupport. Therefore, $L_1 = \{1\},\{2\},\{3\},\{5\}$

We now create C_2 from L_1

$C_2 = \{1,2\},\{1,3\},\{1,5\},\{2,3\},\{2,5\},\{3,5\}$ with support 1, 2, 1, 2, 3 and 2, respectively

Based on the minimum required support:

$L_2 = \{1,3\}, \{2,3\}, \{2,5\}, \{3,5\}$ and $C_3 = \{2,3,5\}$.

C_3 contains only one itemset with support of 2. This then terminates the processes of finding the itemsets.

Given the frequent itemsets, we now create the rules:

The itemset in our case is $C_3=\{2,3,5\}$,

1. The proper non-empty subsets of C_3 are: $\{2,3\},\{2,5\}, \{3,5\}, \{2\}, \{3\}, \{5\}$.
2. The association rules from these subset are:

Rule	Support	Confidence
$\{2,3\} \Rightarrow \{5\}$	50%	100%
$\{2,5\} \Rightarrow \{3\}$	50%	67%
$\{3,5\} \Rightarrow \{2\}$	50%	100%
$\{2\} \Rightarrow \{3,5\}$	50%	67%
$\{3\} \Rightarrow \{2,5\}$	50%	67%
$\{5\} \Rightarrow \{2,3\}$	50%	67%

Table 38 : Apriori sample results

Using a required support level of 50% and a required confidence level of 70%, only 2 rules are left:

193

1. $\{2,3\} \Rightarrow \{5\}$
2. $\{3,5\} \Rightarrow \{2\}$

11.3 Rules Evaluation Criteria

We use four criteria to evaluate rules for their "quality":

- Support - Support of an itemset A is the percent (or number of times) that this itemsets appear in the data. Given the dataset D, the support(A) is defined as Support (A) = count(A) / |D|.

  For an association rule of the form $A \Rightarrow C$ the support is defined as

  Support $(A \Rightarrow C)$ = Support (A union C) = P(AC)

- Confidence - Confidence measure the "strength" of the rule. It is calculated defined as

  Confidence $(A \Rightarrow C)$= Support (A union C) / Support (A) = P(C|A).

- Lift - the Lift of a rule is defined as

  Lift $(A \Rightarrow C)$ = P(C|A) / P(A)

- "Interstingness" – Rule induction algorithm (usually) create a large number of rules from a given dataset. An "interestingness" parameter is defined to choose the "best" rules. The "Interstingness" parameter identifies rules which are helpful and contain new knowledge regarding the problem's domain.

  In this work, we follow the definition of "interstingness" parameters described in [83, 84], which is based on the amount of additional information that each rule contribute. For example: consider the following rules, where about a quarter of people in the age group 20-30 are in the age group 20-25.

  Age(20-30) => Cars(1-2)   8% support, 70% confidence

  Age(20-25) => Cars(1-2)   8% support, 70% confidence

  The second rule can be considered redundant since it does not convey any additional information and is less general than the first rule. Given the first rule, we expect that the second rule would have the same confidence as the first and support equal to quarter of the support for the first. Even if the confidence of the

194

second rule was a little different, say 68% or 73%, it does not convey significantly more information than the first rule. The notion of "interest" is captured by saying that we only want to find rules whose support and/or confidence is greater then expected.

In general, the formal definition of interesting rules is as follows: Given a set of rules S and a minimum interest R, a rule A => C is interesting (in S) if it has no ancestors or it is R-interesting with respect to its close ancestors among its interesting ancestors.

We call $\hat{Z}$ an ancestor of Z (where Z, $\hat{Z}$ are sets of items) if we can get $\hat{Z}$ from Z by replacing one or more items in Z with their ancestors and Z and $\hat{Z}$ have the same number of items.

A rule $A \Rightarrow C$ is called R-interesting w.r.t an ancestor $\hat{A} \Rightarrow \hat{C}$ if the support of the rule $A \Rightarrow C$ is R-times the expected support based on $\hat{A} \Rightarrow \hat{C}$ or the confidence is R times the expected confidence based on $\hat{A} \Rightarrow \hat{C}$.

Based on this interpretation of the "interest level", all rules whose level is higher then a given threshold level will be considered interesting.

The number of association rules that can be derived from a dataset D are exponentially large. "Interesting" association rules are those who:

- Support is greater then a pre-defined minSupport
- Confidence is greater than a pre-defined minConfidence
- Lift values are close to 1 (or 100%)
- Contribute additional information

In this work, we used several cut off points to reduce the number of rules while maintaining the overall performance measure of the rules on the training dataset - the support of the whole set of rules, and the support of all the rule's ascendants.

11.4 Analytical Incremental Apriori

The original Apriori algorithm, which was described in the previous section, is a non-incremental algorithm. The algorithm uses all the samples in order to create the association rules. Therefore, whenever new samples are added, the rules need to be re-calculated using all the former processed samples. We offer now an incremental algorithm for updating the rules as new samples arrive:

1. Get the new observation(s)
2. Update the itemsets support - Update the support of all the itemsets which are relevant to the observation(s):
    a. Update all the itemsets in C_1 according to the observation(s)
    b. Update C_2....C_k in the same way
3. Update the frequent itemsets lists - According to the changes in C_1,....,C_k update L_1,....,L_k
4. Update the rules
    a. For each existing rule, update the confidence and support level
    b. Remove rules whose confidence is lower then MinConfidence or support is lower then MinSupport
    c. From the new itemsets in L_k, add rules that have confidence greater then MinConfidence and support greater then MinSupport

To demonstrate this incremental algorithm, a simple example is used:

Assume that the following data samples were processed (same as in the previous section)

Item set
1,3,4
2,3,5
1,2,3,5
2,5

Table 39 : Incremental Apriori sample data (same as above)

And assume that the MinSupport is 50% of the samples and the MinConfidence is 70%.

The sub-sets and their support are

C_0	Support	C_0	Support	C_0	Support
{1}	2	{2,4}	0	{1,4,5}	0
{2}	3	{2,5}	3	{2,3,4}	0
{3}	3	{3,4}	1	{2,3,5}	2
{4}	1	{3,5}	2	{2,4,5}	0
{5}	3	{4,5}	0	{3,4,5}	0
{1,2}	1	{1,2,3}	0	{1,2,3,4}	0
{1,3}	1	{1,2,4}	0	{1,2,3,5}	1
{1,4}	1	{1,2,5}	1	{1,3,4,5}	0
{1,5}	1	{1,3,4}	1	{2,3,4,5}	0
{2,3}	2	{1,3,5}	1	{1,2,3,4,5}	0

Step #1 – get the new data sample

The sample to process is {1,2,4}.

Step #2 – Update the itemset support

Given the new data sample, the following itemsets needs to be updated

{1}, {2}, {4}, {1,2}, {1,4}, {2,4}, {1,2,4}

So their new support values are

Updated group	Support	Updated group	Support	Updated group	Support
{1}	3	{1,2}	2	{1,2,4}	1
{2}	4	{1,4}	2		
{4}	2	{2,4}	1		

Step #3 – Update the frequent itemsets lists

Therefore, before processing the new data sample we had

L_1	Support	L_2	Support	L_3	Support

197

{1}	2	{1,3}	2	{2,3,5}	2
{2}	3	{2,3}	2		
{3}	3	{2,5}	3		
{5}	3	{3,5}	2		

After processing the new sample we get

L$_1$	Support	L$_2$	Support	L$_3$	Support
{1}	3	{2,5}	3		
{2}	4				
{3}	3				
{5}	3				

{4} was not added since its new support is only 2/5

{1,3}, {2,3}, {3,5} were removed since their support is only 2/5 which is too low

L$_3$ is empty since the support of {2,3,5} is 2/5 so it was removed from the group.

Step #4 – Update the rules

Since {2,3,5} is no longer in L$_3$ then all the rules based on this item sets needs to be removed. In this case the two existing rules "{2,3} $\Rightarrow$ {5}" and "{3,5} $\Rightarrow$ {2}" are removed.

The largest not-empty list of itemset is now L$_2$ = {2,5}, therefore two possible rule are checked:

Rule	Support	Confidence
{2} ⇒ {5}	3/5 = 60%	Support(2,5) / Support (2) = 3 / 4 = 75%
{5} ⇒ {2}	3/5 = 60%	Support (2,5) / Support (5) = 3 / 3 = 100%

Table 40 : Incremental Apriori sample results

The support of both rules is greater then the MinSupport and the confidence level of both rules is grater then MinCondifence, so these two rules are valid and can be used.

This incremental algorithm that for updating association rules as new samples are processed can easily handle cases in which the number of existing items is small (5 in the example above). But in cases where there are many items, like in most data mining problems, this algorithm is very inefficient. In order to process the observation(s) the algorithm need to save the support of all possible itemsets in order to quickly update the support levels whenever new observation(s) arrive. However, in large databases the number of possible itemsets is huge and can not be saved. For example in case with 300 possible items, there are $2^{300} = 2*10^{90}$ possible itemsets. Clearly, no algorithm can save this amount of information.

A possible solution to this could have been to save only the items set with are "suspected" to become frequent. But since in most case we do not know in advance which itemsets will become frequent when more samples arrive, then basically all itemsets are "suspected" to become frequent, and therefore all of them need to be saved.

Consequently, the analytical Apriori algorithm is not feasible for large databases that we usually encounter in real business applications. We offer a cube-based approach for rule induction in order to overcome this limitation.

11.5 The Cube-Based Incremental Apriori Algorithm

The cube-based incremental Apriori algorithm proceeds as follows:

1. Initialization step
    a. Get the boundaries of the problem's space both for the dependent and independent variables. The number of dimensions in the problem's space is marked d.
    b. Decide on the size of the cubes.

2. Update the relevant cube
    c. Get new observation
    d. For each observation $(x_{1,n+1},...,x_{i,n+1},...,x_{d,n+1})$ where $x_{i,j}$ indicates the ith attribute in the jth observation.
        i. Find the cube to which this observation belongs.
        ii. If this cubes has already been used
            then increase the counter for this cube (the only data stored for each cube is the number of data points which are residue inside the cube),
            else create this cube with counter=1

3. Update the itemsets support –
    e. Update C_1 with all the relevant items in the new sample(s)
    f. Find frequent itemsets L_k from C_k –
        i. Add to L_k the itemsets in C_k whose support is greater then the MinSupport,
        ii. Remove from L_k the itemsets whose support is smaller then MinSupport.
    g. Form C_{k+1} from L_k –

i. If both $\{a_1,..,a_{k-2}, a_{k-1}\} \in L_{k-1}$ and

$\{a_1,..., a_{k-2}, a_k\} \in L_{k-1}$, where a_i is an item in an itemset,

then add $\{a_1,..,a_{k-2}, a_{k-1}, a_k\}$ to C_k.

ii. Remove $\{a_1, ...,a_{k-2}, a_{k-1}, a_k\}$, if it contains a non-frequent (k-1) subset.

4. Update the rules

    h. Remove the rule whose support is now smaller then the MinSupport or confidence is smaller then MinConfidence

    i. For all the new frequent itemsets X

        i. For every non-empty subset A of X

        ii. Let $C = X - A$.

        iii. $A \Rightarrow C$ is an association rule if,

        confidence$(A \Rightarrow C) \geq$ minConfidence

        and

        support$(A \Rightarrow C) \geq$ minSupport

5. For each new data arrives, return to step 2.

The difference between this algorithm and one described in the previous section is that this algorithm does not store the support level of all possible itemsets but uses the data stored in the cubes in order to find the support of itemsets. In cases where there are many items, this change dramatically reduced the amount of memory needed by the algorithm as well as the computation time.

11.6 Implementation on a Realistic Dataset

We use the non-profit dataset to test the performance of the cube-based Apriori algorithm and compare the results to those of the original, non-incremental Apriori algorithm.

11.6.1 Original Apriori Results

The original Apriori algorithm was activated on the training data set, using all the predictors in the dataset (no influential predictors have been chosen in advance).
The algorithm created a large number of rules. So we used "interestingness" measures to eliminate non-interesting rules [83, 84].
We checked several cut-off levels to find that the interest level that renders a reasonable amount of rules, with high confidence and support level is "interest level" >= 1, This cut off point yields a very reasonable 28 rules.

The results of the received rules were:

Rule Num.	Original Apriori		
	% Support	% Confidence	% Lift
1	81.68	100.00	97.30
2	81.60	100.00	97.20
3	81.57	100.00	97.16
4	83.30	100.00	97.13
5	81.50	100.00	97.08
6	81.50	100.00	97.08
7	81.49	100.00	97.07
8	81.49	100.00	97.07
9	81.68	100.00	95.24
10	81.60	100.00	95.14
11	81.57	100.00	95.10
12	81.50	100.00	95.03
13	81.50	100.00	95.02
14	81.49	100.00	95.01
15	81.49	100.00	95.01
16	83.30	100.00	94.89
17	81.83	100.00	93.21
18	81.68	100.00	93.05

19	81.60	100.00	92.95
20	81.57	100.00	92.91
21	81.50	100.00	92.84
22	81.50	100.00	92.83
23	81.49	100.00	92.82
24	81.49	100.00	92.82
25	81.61	100.00	85.31
26	81.58	100.00	81.68
27	81.54	100.00	81.56
28	81.51	100.00	81.54

Table 41 : Apriori results

11.6.2 Cube-Based Incremental Apriori Results

To activate the incremental cube-based Apriori algorithm described above, we divided the non profit dataset into 3 groups: the first, 40,000 samples were used in order to create the rules model; the second 10,000 samples were used to incrementally update the model and the balance of the dataset. Then we used 50,000 observations, to validate the model results.

Also in this case, just like in the original Apriori algorithm, all the predictors in the dataset took part in the algorithm (i.e., we did not chose the most influential predictors in advance). The "interestingness" cut-off point was >= 1.001, yielding 30 rules.

The results of the received rules are:

	"Cube-based" Apriori		
Rule Num.	% Support	% Confidence	% Lift
1	85.34	95.77	104.12
2	83.83	97.64	102.28
3	83.71	97.73	102.13
4	83.65	97.73	102.05
5	83.64	97.73	102.04
6	83.63	97.73	102.03
7	83.63	97.73	102.03
8	83.63	97.73	102.03
9	85.34	97.99	101.66
10	83.66	98.29	97.54

11	81.81	100.00	97.46
12	85.34	94.66	95.49
13	83.83	99.76	87.64
14	82.51	99.66	86.26
15	81.94	99.84	85.66
16	81.88	99.84	85.59
17	81.87	99.84	85.59
18	81.86	99.84	85.58
19	81.86	99.84	85.58
20	81.86	99.84	85.58
21	81.86	99.84	85.58
22	83.71	99.90	83.82
23	82.31	99.90	82.41
24	81.94	99.90	82.04
25	81.83	99.90	81.93
26	81.83	99.90	81.93
27	81.81	99.90	81.92
28	81.81	99.90	81.92
29	81.81	99.90	81.92
30	81.81	99.90	81.92

Table 42 : Incremental Apriori results

11.7 Results Analysis

11.7.1 Comparing the Results

The results of the two algorithms described above are summarized in the following table:

	Original Apriori training	Original Apriori validation	"cube-based" Apriori Training	"cube-based" Apriori Validation
Num of Rules	28		30	
Average Support	81.13	81.68	82.28	82.85
Average Confidence	99.98	100.00	98.96	98.94
Average Lift	93.11	93.25	90.51	90.79

Table 43 : Rule induction results comparison - summary

Table 43 indicate that the results obtained with the cube-based incremental Apriori algorithm are very similar to those obtained by the original Apriori algorithm, suggesting that the cube-based approach is a viable alternative for updating knowledge in light of additional observations. Using the cube-based data representation instead of the actual data points seem to have only a small (and negligible) effect on the quality of the model results.

11.7.2 Rules Similarity Comparison

To further examine the similarity between the rules created by these two algorithms, we analyzed in depth five rules which were randomly picked from set of rules above. In Table 44 we list the variables in the antecedent and the consequent parts of each rule:

Original Apriori Algorithm		Cube-based Apriori Algorithm	
Ans.	Cons.	Ans.	Cons.
V66, V69, V70, V71, V129, V134, V139, V144	V68	V69, V70, V71, V129, V134, V139, V144	V68
V68, V69, V70, V71, V129, V134, V139, V144	V66	V68, V69, V70, V71, V134, V139, V144	V129
V63, V66, V69, V71, V129, V134, V139, V144	V70	V69, V71, V129, V134, V139, V144	V70
V63, V66, V69, V70, V129, V134, V139, V144	V71	V68, V69, V70, V129, V134, V139, V144	V71
V63, V66, V68, V69, V70, V71, V139, V153	V144	V68, V69, V70, V71, V139, V144	V153

Table 44 : Rules comparison

We can see from this table that there is a "good" similarity between the rules created by the original Apriori algorithm and the incremental cube-based Apriori algorithm. In general the rules are very similar, but in the cube-based algorithm the condition part of the rule (the antecedent) is usually shorter – due to the difference in the itemsets found by the algorithm.

11.7.3 Predictor Comparison

In the original Apriori algorithm, the frequent itemsets were created by 11 predictors only versus 9 predictors for the cube-based approach, as summarized in Table 45 below:

	Number of predictors
Predictors used by both algorithms	9
Predictors used by the original algorithm but not by the cube-based algorithm	2
Predictors used by the cube-based algorithm but not by the original algorithm	0

Table 45 : Predictors comparison

So even in terms of predictors making up the rules, there appears to be no major difference between the rules based on the original data points and those based on the cube-based data points.

11.8 Conclusions

In this chapter we describe a cube-based incremental approach for rules induction using the Apriori model. Comparing the results obtained with the cube-based approach to the rules created by the original Apriori algorithm reveals no major differences between the rules. This suggests that the cube-based approach for rule induction is a viable approach for updating knowledge for incremental data.

12 Conclusion

In many cases, by the time one builds a data mining model and validates its results, the model is already obsolete as new data continuously keeps coming in. Building a data mining model from large amounts of data requires time and computer resources. On the other hand, new data is easily created, so the need to update existing models based on new data is common.

A solution to this problem is to build an initial model based on the existing data and update this model whenever new data arrives. This work offers an approach for model updates which is general enough and works on all types of data mining models. The approach is based on saving a summary of the data using multi-dimensional cubes. The multi-dimensional problem space is divided into cubes, and for each one we save the cube's location in the problem space and the number of observations in this cube. This allows us to save much less information then the original data, but at the same time have all the necessary (and detailed) information in order to perform accurate data model updates.

In using the cube approach to store summarized data, the process for model updates is to:
1. Use the existing dataset to create the initial model.
2. Convert the existing dataset so as to be represented using cubes.
   i. For each observation in the database (the X matrix), find the cube to which this observation belongs.
   ii. Create the Z matrix which describes which cubes in the problem space have observations in them, and the number each cube includes.
3. As new observations are added, update the Z matrix to accommodate the additional data.
4. When it is the time to update the model, convert the Z matrix into a format the data mining algorithm can use (the W matrix) and apply the algorithm. The W matrix has the same dimensions as the X matrix, but instead of the actual data values, it has the cube location in the problem's space.

The main contribution of this work is the development of a generic method to summarize data for incremental data mining. The existing literature shows several ways to summarize data for data mining algorithms and a few incremental data mining algorithms. This work "combines" these two fields by creating a method to summarize data for incremental data mining. The method described in this work has three main attributes:

1. The saved summarized data is detailed enough to perform accurate data model updates, while at the same time requires a lot less memory than storing the entire data set (1% of the storage needed for the entire dataset). This also means that the data mining algorithms running on the cube data will usually require less computational resources.

2. The method is generic and can be used for all types of data mining algorithms. The existing methods for summarized data described in the literature review have been developed to solve a specific problem, while the approach described here is generic and can be used with any algorithm. We have achieved that by using an approach which is "data based" and not "algorithm based". This approach is actually summarizes the data and is completely not dependent on how the data is going to be used.

3. Easy to use. The creation of the cubes is simple and does not require any complex calculating. On top of that, their use (in order to update the existing model) is simple and does not require major changes in the algorithm.

This work has also addressed the problem of incremental pre-processing. In general, in order for data mining algorithms to produce the best results the data needs to be "pre-processed" before it is sent to the data mining algorithm. In the case of incremental data mining algorithms the "pre-processing" needs to happen as new samples become available and without the ability to review all the samples in advance. This creates some limitation on the operations that can be performed in this stage, and therefore specific methods for pre-processing need to be developed.

To implement the cube method we picked one model from each of the five major class models of data mining – linear regression, logistic regression, classification models (CHAID), clustering models (K-Means) and rule induction (the Apriori algorithm). Overall we found no major difference between the model results for the validation datasets for each of the five class models. This suggests that the cube-based approach constitutes a viable approach, not only for updating knowledge based on incremental data, but it is also for building data mining models from scratch.

These different implementations clearly show the benefits of the cube model. It is easy to use, achieves significant memory savings, the same model can be used for all algorithms, and the results are good.

This work covered different issues related to incremental data mining, but the field of incremental algorithms is very wide with many research questions still unanswered. The following describes some of the issues requiring further study:

- The data mining literature discusses a multitude of algorithms for classification, clustering and rule induction. In this work we only considered one algorithm per each class of model. An interesting research direction is to expand the cube-based approach for other algorithms.

- As this work had to pre-process the data before mining it, the issue of incremental data pre-processing needed to be addressed. As this was not the focus of this work it was only briefly looked at. Further research on this topic is required to make the cube-based approach even more general and to allow it to accommodate all types of new data elements.

- Finally, while we have placed the focus in this work on knowledge updates for data mining, there are several potential avenues of expansion for this approach into other domains, such as fraud detection, internet applications, and search engines.

Additional areas of future work could focus on improving the way the data is summarized for the incremental data mining algorithms. In our case we used multi-dimensional cubes, but the use of other multi-dimensional shapes (like multi-dimensional spheres or multi-dimensional hexagons) should be explored as they might even be more efficient and save additional storing space. Another option for improving the model is to use different sizes of cubes. In our case we split each dimension into equal-sized cubes. As the data is not distributed uniformly, it might be even more beneficial if each dimension was split into different size of cubes dependent on the amount of data points which "fall" into each. This might allow memory savings and obtain even better results in the incremental data mining algorithms.

One of the advantages of the cube model is the flexibility to create cubes of different sizes dependant on the amount of memory that we have and the accuracy of the data that is required. This work has briefly discussed this issue, but future research on the optimal cube size would be helpful when implementing the cubes of new datasets.

Bibliography

[1] Fayyad U., Piatetsky-Shapiro G. and Smyth P. (1996), "The KDD Process for Extracting Useful Knowledge from Volumes of Data", Communications of the ACM, 39(11).

[2] Spiegler I. (2000) "Knowledge Management: A new idea or a recycled concept ?" Communications of the AIS, Volume 3, Article 14, June.

[3] Drucker, P.E. (1995), "The Post Capitalistic Executive" in Drucker P.E.(ed.) Managing in a Time of Great Change, New York, Penguin.

[4] King J. (1993), "Editorial Notes", Information Systems Research, (4)4, pp. 291-298.

[5] Bourdreau A. and Couillard G. (1999), "System Integration and Knowledge Management", Information Systems Management, Fall, pp. 24-32.

[6] Fisher D.H. (1987), "Knowledge acquisition via incremental conceptual clustering", Machine Learning, vol. 2, pp. 139-172.

[7] Lebowitz M. (1987), "Experiments with incremental concept formation: UNIMEM", Machine Learning, vol. 2, pp. 139-172.

[8] Fayyad U., Piatetsky-Shapiro G. and Smyth P. (1996). "From Data Mining to Knowledge Discovery in Databases". AI magazine, Fall.

[9] Draper N.R. and Smith H.(1981) : Applied Regression Analysis, 2nd edition, John Wiley.

[10] Hosmer D.W. and Lemeshow (1989), Applied logistic regression, New York, Wiley.

[11] Kass G. V. (1980), An Exploratory Technique for Investigating Large Quantities of Categorical Data. Applied Statistics vol. 29 pp. 119-127.

[12] Quinlan J.R. (1986), "Induction of Decision Trees", Machine Learning, vol. 1, pp. 81-106.

[13] Shannon, C.E. and Weaver, W. (1949), The Mathematical Theory of Communication, U. of Illinois Press, Urbana, Ill.

[14] Schlimmer, J. C. and Fisher, D. (1986), "A case study of incremental concept induction". Proceeding of the fifth national conference on Artificial Intelligence, Philadelphia, PA, Morgan Kaufmann, pp. 496-501.

[15] Hunt, E., Marin, J., & Stone, P. (1966). Experiments in induction. New York: Academic Press.

[16] Michalski R.S. and Larson J.B. (1978), "Selection of most representative training examples and incremental generation of VL1 hypotheses: The underlying methodology and the description of the programs ESEL and AQ11", Tech. Rep. No. UIUCDCS-R-78-867, Urbana, University of Illinois, Department of computer Science.

[17] Michalski R.S. (1973). "Discovering classification rules using variable valued logic system VL1 ."Proceedings of the Third Intl. Joint Conf. on Artificial Intelligence, Stanford, CA, Morgan Kaufmann, pp.162-172.

[18] Reinke R.E. and Michalki R.S. (1986). "Incremental learning of concept descriptions ,"Machine Intelligence, vol. 11, Oxford University Press.

[19] Silverman B.W., Jones M.C. , Fix E. and Hodges J.I. (1989), "An Important Contribution to Nonparametric Discriminant Analysis and Density Estimation -

Commentary on Fix and Hodges" (1951). International Statistical Review, 57(3), pp. 233-247.

[20] Ng R. T. and Han J. (1994), "Efficient and effective clustering methods for spatial data mining", VLDB.

[21] Goha S., Rastogu R., and Shim K. (1998), "Cure: An efficient clustering algorithm for large databases". Proceedings of the ACM SIGMOD.

[22] Jain A.K., Murty M.N. and Flyyn P.J. (1999), "Data Clustering: A review", ACM Computing Surveys (CSUR), 31(3).

[23] Feigenbaum E. A. (1963), "The simulation of verbal learning behaviour". In Feigenbaum E. A. and Feldman J. ed. ,Computer and thought, McGraw-Hill, New York.

[24] Zhang T., Ramakrishnan R. and Livny M. (1996), "BIRCH: an efficient data clustering method for very large databases". Proceedings of the ACM SIGMOD international conference on Management of data, pp. 103 - 114.

[25] Nevins A.J. (1995), "A Branch and Bound Incremental Conceptual Clusterer", Machine learning, vol. 18, pp. 5-22.

[26] MacQueen J. B (1967), "Some Methods for classification and Analysis of Multivariate Observations, Proceedings of 5-th Berkeley Symposium on Mathematical Statistics and Probability", Berkeley, University of California Press, vol. 1, pp. 281-297

[27] Mannila H, Toivonen H, Verkamo AI (1994). "Efficient algorithms for discovering association rules." AAAI Workshop on Knowledge Discovery in Databases (SIGKDD), pp. 181-92

[28] Shiby T., Sreenath B., Khaled A., and Sanjay R. (1997), "An efficient algorithm for the incremental updating of association rules in large databases", In Proceedings of the 3rd International conference on Knowledge Discovery and Data Mining (KDD 97), New Port Beach, California.

[29] Clark P. and Niblett T. (1989), "The CN2 induction algorithm", Machine Learning, 3(4), pp.261-284, March.

[30] Date C. J. (2000), An Introduction to Data Base Systems, 6th Edition, Addison Wesley.

[31] S. Guha, N. Koudas, K. Shim (2001). Data Streams and Histograms. Proceedings of the thirty-third annual ACM symposium on Theory of computing. July 2001.

[32] Y. Ioannidis (1993). Universality of Serial Histograms. Proceedings of VLDB, pages 256-277, 1993.

[33] Y. Ioannidis and S. Chrisodoulakis (1993). Optimal Histograms for Limiting Worst-Case Error Progaration in the Size of Join Results. ACM Trnsactions on Database Systems, Vol. 18, No. 4, pages 709-748, December 1993.

[34] Y. Ioannidis and V. Poosala (1999). Histogram Based Approximation of Set Query Answers. Proceedings of VLDB, pages 174-185, 1999.

[35] Y. Ioannidis and V. Poosala (1995). Balancing Histogram Optimality and Practicality for Query Result Size Estimation. Proceeding of the ACM SIGMOD, 1995.

[36] H. V. Jagadish, N. Koudas, S. Muthukrishnan, V. Poosala, K. C. Sevcik and T. Suel (1998). Optimal Histograms with Quality Guarantees. Proceedings of VLDB, 1998.

[37] N. Koudas, S. Muthukrishnan and D. Srivastava (2000). Optimal histograms for heirarchical range queries. Proceeding of <u>ACM PODS</u>, 2000.

[38] Y. matias, J. Scott Vitter and M.Wang (1998). Wavelet-Based Histograms for Selectivity Estimation. Proceeding of <u>ACM SIGMOD</u>, 1998.

[39] M. Muralikrishna and D. J. Dewitt (1998). Equi-depth histograms for estimating selectivity factors for multidimentional queries. Proceedings of ACM SIGMOD, 1998.

[40] M. Muralikrishna, V. Poosala and T. Suel (1999) On Rectangular Partitioning In Two Dimentions: Algorithms, Complexity and Applications. Proceedings of ICDT, 1999.

[41] V. Poosala and Y. Ioannidis (1996). Estimation of Query-Result Distribution and its Application In Parallel Join Load Balancing. Proceeding of VLDB, 1996.

[42] V. Poosala and Y. Ioannidis (1997). Selectivity estimation without the attribute value independence assumption. Proceeding of VLDB, 1997.

[43] V. Poosala, Y. Ioannidis, P. Haas and E. Shekita (1996). Improved Histogram for Selectivity Estimation of Range Predicates. Proceedings of ACM SIGMOD, 1996.

[44] A. Acharya, P. Gibbons, V. Poosala and S. Ramaswamy (1999). Join Synopses For Approximate Query Answering. Proceedings of ACM SIGMOD, pages 275-186, June 1999.

[45] A. Acharya, P. Gibbons, V. Poosala and S. Ramaswamy (1999). The Aqua Approximate Query Answering System. Prceedings of ACM SIGMOD, pages 574-578, June 1999.

[46] P. Gibbons, Y. Mattias and V. Poosala (2002). Fast Incremental Maintenance of Approximate Histograms. ACM Transcations on Database Systems, Vol. 27, No. 3, Sep. 2002.

[47] V. Poosala and V. Ganti (1999). Fast Approximate Answers To Aggregate Queries On A Datacube. SSDBM, pages 24-33, 1999.

[48] J. Vitter and M. Wang (1999) Approximate computation of multidimentional aggregates on sparse data using wavelets. Proceedings of ACM SIGMOD, 1999.

[49] J. Vitter, W. Wang and B. R. Iyer (1998) Data Cube Approximation and Histograms via Wavelets. Proceedings of the 1998 ACM CIKM Intern. Conf. on Information and Knowledge Management, 1998.

[50] H. V. Jadadish, N. Koudas and S. Muthukrishnan (1999). Mining Deviants in a Time Series Database. Proceeding of VLDB, 1999.

[51] M. Berlotto and M. J. Egenhofer (1999). Progressive vector transmission. Proceedings of the 7th ACM symposium on Advance in Geographical Information Systems, 1999.

[52] Y. Ioannidis (1997). Query optimization. In <u>Handbook for Computer Science</u>. CRC press, 1997.

[53] Kooi, R. P. (1980). The optimization of queries in relational database. PhD thesis. Case Western Reserve University

[54] N. Bruno, S. Chaudhuri and L. Gravano (2001). STHoles: A Multidimensional Worload-Aware Hstogram. ACM SIGMOD 2001.

[55] Y. Ioannidis and V. Poosala (1999). Histogram-based approximation of set-valued query-answers. In VLDB 1999.

[56] N. Thaper, P. Indyk, S. Guha and N. Koudas (2002). Dynamic Multidimensional histograms. ACM SIGMOD 2002.

[57] Y. Ioannidis and S. Christodoulakis (1993). Optimal Histogram for Limiting Worst-Case Error Propogation in the Size of Joing Results. ACM trans. on database systems. 18(4) pages 709-748, 1993.

[58] Codd E. F. (1970). A relational model of data for large shared data banks, Communications of the ACM. Volume 13 , Issue 6, pp. 377 - 387

[59] Vassiliadis P. and Sellis T. K. (1999). " A Survey of Logical Models for OLAP Databases". SIGMOD Record vol. 28 num. 4 pp. 64-69

[60] OLAP council (1997). The APB-1 Benchmark. Available at http://www.olapcouncil.org/research/bmarkly.htm

[61] Gray L., Bosworth A., Layman A. and Pirahesh H. (1996). "Data cube: A relational aggregation operator generalizing group-by, cross-tab and sub-totals". Proceedings of the ICDE.

[62] Li C. and Wang X. S. (1996). "A data model for supporting on-line analytical processings. CIKM.

[63] Gyssens M. and Lakshmanan L.V.S. (1997). "A foundation for multi-dimensional databases". 23rd VLDB Conference.

[64] Gingras F. and Lakshmanan L. (1998). "nD-SQL: A Multi-dimensional Languge for Interoperability and OLAP". Proceedings of the 24th VLDB Conference.

[65] Agrawal R., Gupta A. and Sarawagi S. (1995). Modeling Multidimensional Databases. IBM Research Report, Sept. 1995.

[66] Cabbibo L. and Torlone R. (1997). "Querying Multidimensional Databases". 6th DBPL Workshop.

[67] Vassiliadis P. (1998). "Modeling Multidimensional Databases, Cubes and Cube Operations". 10th SSDBM Conference.

[68] Lehner W. (1998). "Modeling large scale OLAP scenarios". 6th EDBT.

[69] Lehner W., Albrect J. and Wedekind H. (1998). "Normal Forms for Multidimensional Databases". 10th SSDBM Conference.

[70] Bellman, R.E. 1961. Adaptive Control Processes. Princeton University Press, Princeton, NJ.

[71] Jimenez L. and Landgrebe D. (1997). "Supervised Classification in High Dimenisonal Space: Geometrical, Statistical and Asymptotical Properties for Multuvariate Data". IEEE Transactions on Systems, Man and Cybernetics. Vol. 28 part C num. 1, pp. 39-54

[72] Havil G. J. (2003). "Exploring Euler's Constant". Princeton, NJ: Princeton University Press.

[73] Two crows web site. http://www.twocrows.com/

[74] Garofalakis G., Gehrke J. and Rastogi R (2002). Querying and Mining Data Streams: You Only Get One Look. Proceedings of the 2002 ACM SIGMOD international conference on Management of data. Tutorial session. pp. 635 - 635

[75] Ioannidis Y. E. and Poosala V (1999). Historagram based Approcimation of Set-Valued Query Answers. VLDB.

[76] Lambert P. J. nad Aronson R. J. (1993). Inequality Decomposition Analysis and the Gini Coefficient Revisited. The Economic Journal, 103, pp. 1221-1227

[77] Chakravarti, Laha, and Roy, (1967). Handbook of Methods of Applied Statistics, Volume I, John Wiley and Sons, pp. 392-394

[78] Levin N. and Zahavi J. (2005). "GainSmart Data Mining System for Marketing".

[79] Ben-Akiva M and Lerman S. R. (1985). *Discrete Choice Analysis*. Cambridge: MIT Press.

[80] Huang Z (1998). Extensions to the k-Means Algorithm for Clustering Large Data Sets with Categorical Values. Data mining and Knowledge Discovery, vol. 2 pp 283-304.

[81] L. Bobrowski L. and Bezdek J. C.(1991). "C-means clustering with the L1 and L00 norms",IEEE Transactions on Systems Man and Cybernetics, Vol. 21, No. 3., pp. 545-554.

[82] Agrawal R. and Srikant R. (1994). "Fast Algorithms for Mining Association Rules". Proc. 20th Int. Conf. VLDB, pp. 487-499

[83] Srikant R. and Agrawal R. (1996). "Mining Quantitative Association rules in Large Relational Tables" Proceedings of the 1996 ACM SIGMOD International Conference on Management of Data, pp. 1-12

[84] Srikant R. and Agrawal R. (1997). "Mining generalized association rules". Future Generation Computer Systems, pp.161-180.

[85] Utgoff P. E. (1989). "Incremental induction of decision trees". Machine learning, 4, pp. 161-186.

[86] Kalles D. and Morris T. (1995). "Efficient Incrmental Induction of Decision Trees". Machine Learning, 1, pp.1-13.

[87] V. Dhar & A. Tuzhilin (1993). "Abstract Driven Pattern Discovery in Databases". IEEE Transactions on Knowledge and Data Engineering, Volume 5 , Issue 6, pp 926 – 938, December 1993.

[88] J. Han (1998), " Towards On-Line Analytical Mining in Large Databases", SIGMOD Record, 27(1):97-107, 1998.

[89] J. Han, J Wang, G. Dong, J. Pei & K. Wang (2002). "Cube Explorer : Online Exploration of Data Cubes". ACM SIGMOD 2002.

[90] D. Xin and J. Han "P-Cube: Answering Preference Queries in Multi-Dimensional Space", Proc. 2008 Int. Conf. on Data Engineering (ICDE'08), Cancun, Mexico, April 2008.

[91] J. Han and S. Chee and J. Chiang "Issues for On-Line Analytical Mining of Data Warehouses (Extended Abstract)". "citeseer.ist.psu.edu/17942.html"

[92] J. Han and Y. Fu (1996). "Exploration of the power of attribute-oriented induction in data mining" In U.M. Fayyad, G. Piatetsky-Shapiro, P. Smyth and R. Uthurusamy, editors, Advances is Knowledge Discovery and Data Mining, pp. 399-421. AAAI/MIT press, 1996. [97]

[93] M. Kamber, L. Winstone, W. Gong, S. Cheng and J. Han (1997). "Generalization and decision tree induction: Efficient classification in data mining". Proc of 1997 Int Workshop Research Issues on Data Engineering (RIDE 97), pp. 111-120. April 1997.

[94] M. Kamber, J. Han and J. Y. Chiang (1997). "Metarule-guided mining of multi-dimentional association rules". Proc. 3rd Int. Conf. Knowledge Discovery and Data Mining (KDD 97). Pp 207-210. August 1997.

[95] S. Cheng. "Statistical Approaches to Predictive Modeling in Large Databases". M. Sc. Thesis. January 1998.

[96] R. Agarwal, J. Gehrke, D. Gunopulos and P. Raghavan (1998). "Automatic Subspace clustering of high dimentional data for data mining applications". Proc. 1998 ACM SIGMOD Int. Conf. Managament of Data, June 1998

[97] U.M. Fayyad, G. Piatetsky-Shapiro, P. Smyth and R. Uthurusamy, editors, Advances is Knowledge Discovery and Data Mining, pp. 399-421. AAAI/MIT press, 1996.

[98] J. Han, N. Stefanovic, and K. Koperski, (1998) " Selective Materialization: An Efficient Method for Spatial Data Cube Construction", Proc. 1998 Pacific-Asia Conf. on Knowledge Discovery and Data Mining (PAKDD'98) April 1998

[99] Dong Xin, Jiawei Han, Hong Cheng, and Xiaolei Li (2006), "Answering Top-k Queries with Multi-Dimensional Selections: The Ranking Cube Approach", in Proc. 2006 Int. Conf. on Very Large Data Bases (VLDB'06), Seoul, Korea, Sept. 2006.

[100] O. R. Zaiane, M. Xin, J. Han (1998), " Discovering Web Access Patterns and Trends by Applying OLAP and Data Mining Technology on Web Logs", Proc. Advances in Digital Libraries Conf. (ADL'98), Santa Barbara, CA, April 1998, pp. 19-29

[101] M. Kamber, J. Han, J. Y. Chiang, " Using Data Cubes for Metarule-Guided Mining of Multi-Dimensional Association Rules", Techical Report CS-TR 97-10, School of Computing Science, Simon Fraser University, May 1997.

[102] X. Li, J. Han, and H. Gonzalez, "High-Dimensional OLAP: A Minimal Cubing Approach", Proc. 2004 Int. Conf. on Very Large Data Bases (VLDB'04), Toronto, Canada, Aug. 2004.

[103] J. Gary, S. Chaudhuri, A. Bosworth, A. Layman, D. Reichart, M. Venkatrao, F. Pellow and H. Pirahesh (1997). "Data Cube: A Relational Aggregation Operator Generalizing Group-By, Cross-Tab and Sub-Totals". Data Mining and Knowledge Discovery, 1:29-54, 1997.

[104] J. Han, J. Pei, G. Dong, and K. Wang (2001), " Efficient Computation of Iceberg Cubes with Complex Measures ", Proc. 2001 ACM-SIGMOD Int. Conf. on Management of Data (SIGMOD'01), Santa Barbara, CA, May 2001.

[105] K. Beyer and R. Ramakrishnan. (1999). "Bottom-up computation of sparse and iceberg cubes". SIGMOD 1999.

[106] L. V. S. Lakshmanan, J. Pei, and J. Han (2002), " Quotient Cube: How to Summarize the Semantics of a Data Cube ", Proc. 2002 Int. Conf. on Very Large Data Bases (VLDB'02), Hong Kong, China, Aug. 2002.

[107] G. Sathe and S. Sarawagi. (2001). "Intelligent Rollups in Multi-dimensional OLAP data". VLDB 2001, pp. 531-540.

[108] Y. Sismanis, A. Deligiannakis, N. Roussopoulos and Y. Kotidis (2002). DWARF: Shrinking and Petacube. SIGMOD 2002

[109] W. Wang and J. Feng (2002). Condense cube: An effective approach to reducing data cube size. ICDE 2002.

[110] J. Han and Y. Fu (1999). "Mining Multiple-Level Association Rules in Large Databases". IEEE Transactions on Knowledge and Data Engineering. Vol. 11, No.5, 1999.

[111] R. Agrawal, T. Imielinski and A. Swami (1993). "Mining assocication Rules Between Sets of Items in Large Databases". Proc 1993 ACM SIGMOD.

[112] R. Agrawal and J.C. Shafer, (1996). "Parallel Mining of Association Rules: Design, Implementation and Experince". IEEE Trans. Knwoledge and Data Eng. Vol. 8, pp. 962-969, 1996.

[113] R. Agrawal and R. Srikant (1995). "Mining Sequential Patterns". Proc. 1995 Int'l Conf. Data Eng.

[114] D.W. Cheung, J. Han, N. Ng, A. Fu and Y. Fu (1996). "A fast Distributed Algorithm for Mining Association Rules". Proc. 1996 Int'l Conf. Parallel and Distributed Information systems.

[115] D.W. Cheung, J. Han, V. Ng and C.Y. Wong (1996). "Maintenance of Discovered Association Rules in Large Databases: An Incremental Updating Technique". Proc. 1996 Int'l Conf. Data Eng.

[116] Y. Fu and J. Han (1995). "Meta-Rule-Guided Mining of Association Rules in Relational Databases". Proc. First Int'l Workshop Integration Knowledge Discovery with Deductive and Object Oriented Databases (KDOOD '95).

[117] T. Fukuda, Y. Morimoto, S. Morishita and T. Tokuyama (1996). "Data Mining Using Two-Dimensional Optimized Association Rules: Scheme, Algorithms and Visualization". Proc. 1996 ACM SIGMOD Int'l Conf. Management of Data.

[118] M. Houtsuma and A. Swami (1995). "Set Oriented Mining for Association Rules in Relational Databases". Proc. 1995 Int'l Conf. Data Eng.

[119] M. Klemettinen, H. Mannila, P. Ronkainen, H. Toivonen and A.I. Verkamo (1994). "Finding Interesting Rules from Large Sets of Discovered Association Rules". Proc Third Int'l Conf. Information and Knowledge Management 1994.

[120] K. Koperski and J. Han (1995). "Discovery of Spatial Association Rules in Geographic Information Databases". Proc. Forth Int'l Symp. Large Spatial Databases (SSD '95)

[121] H. Mannila, H. Toivonen and A.I. Verkamo (1994). "Efficient Algorithm for Discovering Association Rules". Proc. AAAI '94 Workshop Knowledge Discovery in Databases (KDD '94)

[122] R. Meo, G. Psaila and S. Ceri (1996). "A new SQL-Like Operator for Mining Association Rules". Proc 1996 Int'l Conf Very Large Data Bases.

[123] G. Piatetsky-Shapiro (1991). "Discovery, Analysis and Presentation of Strong Rules". Knowledge Discovery in DataBases, G. Piatetsky-Shapiro and W.J. Frawley, AAAI / MIT press.

[124] A. Savasere, E. Omiecinski and S. Navathe (1995). "An Efficient Algorithm for Mining Association Rules in Large Databases". Proc. 1995 Int'l Conf. Very Large Data Bases.

[125] Proc. Second Int'l Conf. Knowledge Discovery and Data Mining (KDD '96), E. Simoudis, J. Han and U. Fayyad, editors, AAAI press.

[126] R. Srikant and R. Agrawal. (1996). "Mining Quantitative Association Rules in Large Relational Tables". Proc. 1996 ACM SIGMOD.

[127] J. Han, Y. Cai and N. Cercone (1993), " Data-Driven Discovery of Quantitative Rules in Relational Databases ", IEEE Transactions on Knowledge and Data Engineering, 5(1):29-40, 1993.

[128] J. Han and Y. Fu (1994), " Dynamic Generation and Refinement of Concept Hierarchies for Knowledge Discovery in Databases", AAAI'94 Workshop on Knowledge Discovery in Databases (KDD'94), Seattle, WA, July 1994, pp. 157-168.

[129] J. Han, J. Chiang, S. Chee, J. Chen, Q. Chen, S. Cheng, W. Gong, M. Kamber, K. Koperski, G. Liu, Y. Lu, N. Stefanovic, L. Winstone, B. Xia, O. R. Zaiane, S. Zhang, H. Zhu (1997). "DBMiner: A System for Data Mining in Relational Databases and Data Warehouses", Proc. CASCON'97: Meeting of Minds, Toronto, Canada, November 1997.

[130] S. Berchtold, C. Bohm, D. Keim and H.P. Kriegel (1997)" A cost model for nearest neighbout search in high dimensional data space". In Proc. Of the 16th Symposium on Principles of Database Systems (PODS).

[131] J. Friedman (1997). "Optimizating a nosiy function of many variables with application to data mining". In UM/MSR Summer Research Institute in Data Mining.

[132] J. R. Quinlan. (1993) "C4.5: Programs for Machine Learning". Morgan Kaufman, 1993.

[133] J. Dougherty, Kohavi and M. Sahami (1995). "Supervised and unsupervised discretization of continuous features". Proceedings of the Twelfth International Conference on Machine Learning (pp. 194--202). Tahoe City, CA.

[134] Y. Yang and G. Webb (2002). "Discretization for naive-bayes learning: managing discretization bias and variance", In proceedings of PKAW 2002. The 2002 Pacific Rim Knowledge Acquisition Workshop, Tokyo, Japan, pp. 159-173

[135] J. Gama, L. Torgo and C. Soares (1998). "Dynamic discretization of continuous attributes". In Proceedings of the Sixth Ibero-American Conference on AI (1998), pp. 160--169.

Appendix 1- Clustering Detailed Results

Original algorithm training clusters

V1		Mean	N	Std. Deviation	Maximum	% of Total N
	0	748.5	6	210.0836	996	0.012097
	1	1104.054	92	245.5677	1773	0.185484
	2	292.7799	954	47.48855	727	1.923387
	3	222.7908	4876	38.71082	571	9.830645
	4	160.6304	717	50.99596	584	1.445565
	5	88.63415	82	48.81801	264	0.165323
	6	851.1229	301	280.4803	1984	0.606855
	7	1117.313	230	213.1729	1901	0.46371
	8	1005.828	366	284.353	1877	0.737903
	9	801.132	197	186.7513	1534	0.397177
	10	569.9409	558	102.5285	1077	1.125
	11	680.8042	286	274.6445	1770	0.576613
	12	653.2282	425	174.5487	1437	0.856855
	13	86.59756	164	63.38844	358	0.330645
	14	247.2414	116	169.2551	915	0.233871
	15	485.25	80	191.8549	1147	0.16129
	16	786.4919	248	225.1696	1638	0.5
	17	83.44099	161	56.74282	512	0.324597
	18	799.3851	148	178.6386	1476	0.298387
	19	643.2453	53	190.2728	1143	0.106855
	20	168.3146	515	56.20306	459	1.038306
	21	234.9733	2882	55.82276	1063	5.810484
	22	922.9154	260	219.1213	1684	0.524194
	23	311.949	1000	86.19969	947	2.016129
	24	812.5972	216	195.9432	1683	0.435484
	25	773.6522	161	147.4669	1301	0.324597
	26	305.9607	2927	72.17857	742	5.90121
	27	429.9218	1445	172.6146	1228	2.913306
	28	142.3295	264	59.12127	542	0.532258
	29	742.0594	202	176.6069	1537	0.407258
	30	686.6287	509	174.7836	1310	1.02621
	31	715.0741	891	244.1903	1756	1.796371
	32	702.8863	475	206.2758	1486	0.957661
	33	764.6515	66	244.6768	1654	0.133065
	34	329.548	281	179.513	1089	0.566532
	35	931.9058	191	192.019	1638	0.385081
	36	672.7319	235	180.363	1267	0.47379
	37	644.3684	114	198.5454	1410	0.229839
	38	730.1414	474	205.92	1720	0.955645
	39	885.173	185	217.5859	1685	0.372984
	40	782.5049	204	204.0208	1703	0.41129
	41	684.1883	409	167.2492	1372	0.824597

42	626.6009	213	109.832	1223	0.429435
43	763.6796	206	211.441	1434	0.415323
44	191.1608	143	77.62293	705	0.288306
45	373.9559	340	133.3991	1080	0.685484
46	325.1875	96	178.7543	1041	0.193548
47	891.5357	252	191.4857	1692	0.508065
48	718.6544	379	245.2304	1709	0.764113
49	670.2287	328	170.8176	1351	0.66129
50	728.0222	406	231.9365	1541	0.818548
51	443.3004	446	162.5988	988	0.899194
52	365.3085	1021	175.2571	1154	2.058468
53	758.4183	514	152.3645	1722	1.03629
54	165.3192	473	60.61036	735	0.953629
55	379.1597	313	151.0506	1031	0.631048
56	372.8862	378	111.7538	835	0.762097
57	944.9543	481	202.1742	1788	0.969758
58	795.3351	185	219.965	1424	0.372984
59	838.015	133	177.1287	1479	0.268145
60	782.8483	290	155.3943	1679	0.584677
61	824.1513	152	202.2809	1419	0.306452
62	518.5751	353	166.956	1233	0.711694
63	1357.831	65	219.9212	1971	0.131048
64	539.2885	305	167.5106	1350	0.614919
65	696.0858	233	294.4919	1816	0.469758
66	621.9767	172	148.6342	1455	0.346774
67	752.0792	202	192.4083	1465	0.407258
68	823.2706	303	189.6999	1506	0.610887
69	685.4813	214	153.9434	1395	0.431452
70	785.175	200	248.7556	1897	0.403226
71	659.9301	143	289.557	1543	0.288306
72	624.6242	306	165.1167	1659	0.616935
73	731.5863	249	194.9961	1268	0.502016
74	740.1754	114	318.0666	1747	0.229839
75	678.3832	107	242.594	1750	0.215726
76	654.6294	170	174.1809	1291	0.342742
77	660.991	111	189.8373	1444	0.22379
78	985.3103	174	248.1929	1683	0.350806
79	781.7979	292	166.6524	1613	0.58871
80	743.7888	412	173.2948	1775	0.830645
81	594.6214	206	172.8967	1380	0.415323
82	700.8629	175	181.148	1230	0.352823
83	318.8011	186	126.8102	753	0.375
84	584.6415	159	142.3633	1376	0.320565
85	621.5367	300	145.7107	1089	0.604839
86	468.125	24	171.4877	824	0.048387
87	876.2128	639	195.7256	1941	1.288306
88	592.0435	667	170.7812	1204	1.344758
89	275.6	5637	59.25382	689	11.36492
90	486.2543	1101	137.4201	1247	2.219758
91	305.0746	697	128.9165	962	1.405242

92	684.9585	241	197.7582	1263	0.485887
93	567.6588	170	172.5731	1137	0.342742
94	915.2811	217	225.5734	1719	0.4375
95	319.9541	1832	79.37562	761	3.693548
96	163.6476	227	77.76427	950	0.457661
97	730.8022	182	185.9511	1443	0.366935
98	412.5233	1502	122.0877	1067	3.028226
99	339.199	598	133.6118	932	1.205645
Total	457.205	49600	277.7755	1984	100

Original algorithm validation clusters

V1	Mean	N	Std. Deviation	Maximum	% of Total N
0	1719.875	8	488.2717	2453	0.016162
1	1441.304	92	196.2523	2035	0.185859
2	298.6953	1014	47.34264	721	2.048485
3	225.2925	4876	37.97562	635	9.850505
4	158.9507	690	46.00742	351	1.393939
5	100.25	76	54.46764	267	0.153535
6	1418.371	278	265.1026	2622	0.561616
7	1618.968	188	206.5245	2567	0.379798
8	1548.255	298	229.0877	2340	0.60202
9	1263.218	202	176.1324	1958	0.408081
10	625.4026	544	111.9449	1287	1.09899
11	1279.765	247	268.2998	2359	0.49899
12	940.4758	393	166.4986	1560	0.793939
13	94.37647	170	69.07144	481	0.343434
14	321.505	101	162.4252	773	0.20404
15	743.4198	81	216.6401	1537	0.163636
16	1106.009	228	253.1546	1767	0.460606
17	88.39884	173	58.40185	451	0.349495
18	1351.727	139	164.9048	2085	0.280808
19	1236.474	57	147.2203	1521	0.115152
20	172.7653	507	59.29135	473	1.024242
21	240.5709	2834	51.96959	729	5.725253
22	1330.571	280	185.6413	1936	0.565657
23	322.1923	1014	89.8058	1080	2.048485
24	1255.412	260	187.0699	2044	0.525253
25	1101.168	149	173.9929	1935	0.30101
26	315.2387	3054	77.0559	1305	6.169697
27	460.1096	1496	174.4644	1194	3.022222
28	150.1953	256	63.10589	503	0.517172
29	842.8739	222	142.462	1472	0.448485
30	1009.057	473	203.9981	2121	0.955556
31	1291.762	924	216.9574	2308	1.866667
32	1086.257	432	187.1217	1884	0.872727
33	976.087	69	208.888	1716	0.139394
34	454.3493	292	181.3421	1207	0.589899
35	1449.699	176	213.6078	2229	0.355556

36	987.8062	227	186.2141	1688	0.458586
37	910.8273	110	182.2637	1532	0.222222
38	1076.998	490	201.8085	1857	0.989899
39	1377.191	204	246.6127	2170	0.412121
40	1148.087	172	218.6696	2058	0.347475
41	1000.488	367	164.0506	1705	0.741414
42	933.5231	195	92.73492	1216	0.393939
43	1079.861	173	207.3859	1912	0.349495
44	187.4895	143	74.24312	622	0.288889
45	480.3132	348	144.7882	1135	0.70303
46	387.494	83	138.1443	952	0.167677
47	1461.576	231	166.9689	2135	0.466667
48	1298.883	368	222.5715	2124	0.743434
49	948.7026	343	173.677	1654	0.692929
50	1271.992	376	192.0493	2141	0.759596
51	534.7707	458	161.9172	1245	0.925253
52	404.9474	988	190.5935	1278	1.99596
53	1335	402	131.2236	2158	0.812121
54	172.696	500	59.07656	611	1.010101
55	483.6596	376	131.0039	1162	0.759596
56	453.6267	442	133.6383	1310	0.892929
57	1535.732	473	172.9034	2377	0.955556
58	1035.802	167	246.6921	2016	0.337374
59	1113.805	128	179.1811	1791	0.258586
60	1325.382	304	159.1342	2040	0.614141
61	1228.637	201	228.0435	2152	0.406061
62	616.4023	343	187.3393	1375	0.692929
63	1838.873	63	233.0034	2580	0.127273
64	638.2236	322	162.6937	1431	0.650505
65	1230.498	221	265.4074	2186	0.446465
66	907.7095	179	149.0255	1647	0.361616
67	864.1602	206	214.3831	1846	0.416162
68	1358.267	337	178.7308	2052	0.680808
69	964.8729	236	165.5078	1695	0.476768
70	1282.374	195	314.2923	3331	0.393939
71	1227.738	130	238.1456	2095	0.262626
72	955.2635	296	187.0301	1753	0.59798
73	893.8066	243	191.4531	1542	0.490909
74	1077.025	119	294.9093	2176	0.240404
75	1033.579	107	276.3321	2151	0.216162
76	922.513	154	166.8969	1451	0.311111
77	1009.315	124	203.5863	1710	0.250505
78	1530.438	146	244.9248	2185	0.294949
79	1385.287	272	142.7443	2046	0.549495
80	1358.39	341	161.4344	1958	0.688889
81	900.712	191	199.0114	1621	0.385859
82	1115.159	170	218.1248	1870	0.343434
83	384.9263	190	157.34	1469	0.383838
84	858.8079	151	156.8227	1507	0.305051
85	911.1115	287	162.4599	1709	0.579798

86	724.3	20	176.1044	1116	0.040404
87	1419.177	648	186.8126	2692	1.309091
88	846.8685	616	158.9697	1343	1.244444
89	276.9806	5872	59.3774	704	11.86263
90	496.3121	1112	142.3176	1106	2.246465
91	372.6842	722	129.8018	1008	1.458586
92	893.45	240	172.1507	1322	0.484848
93	742.4775	178	214.3696	1556	0.359596
94	1486.071	182	205.0581	2178	0.367677
95	332.1768	1827	79.68432	779	3.690909
96	162.0049	206	54.25886	406	0.416162
97	907.3017	179	202.2247	1877	0.361616
98	432.3991	1511	131.7246	1138	3.052525
99	410.7309	602	140.0202	965	1.216162
Total	601.7214	49500	450.9947	3331	100

Incremental "cube-based" algorithm training clusters

V1		Mean	N	Std. Deviation	Maximum	% of Total N
	0	857.5714	7	236.7515	1238	0.014113
	1	763.5265	359	214.7204	1550	0.72379
	2	298.7351	4741	54.20713	1108	9.558468
	3	222.5523	4775	38.8706	694	9.627016
	4	207.7351	555	89.92339	665	1.118952
	5	175.3902	123	71.53832	346	0.247984
	6	802.3806	268	242.9591	1895	0.540323
	7	1016.28	164	209.5337	1808	0.330645
	8	753.384	750	192.3879	1764	1.512097
	9	867.1667	144	223.3175	1912	0.290323
	10	507.0192	677	130.9572	1193	1.364919
	11	762.3341	449	247.3363	1544	0.905242
	12	775.0643	140	210.8709	1395	0.282258
	13	186.1418	282	66.64231	447	0.568548
	14	265.8894	235	148.9164	879	0.47379
	15	814.1133	256	167.9417	1638	0.516129
	16	858.9856	277	167.9961	1488	0.558468
	17	186.7984	258	90.41572	606	0.520161
	18	821.4615	117	211.4934	1570	0.235887
	19	787.2136	206	204.9666	1783	0.415323
	20	177.1157	527	71.46415	498	1.0625
	21	208.2202	336	91.18555	595	0.677419
	22	857.7012	328	226.5178	1702	0.66129
	23	284.6774	1144	82.93631	771	2.306452
	24	842.9901	101	210.7052	1382	0.203629
	25	624.7826	23	104.8197	873	0.046371
	26	186.873	433	66.80455	582	0.872984
	27	350.8995	1303	92.80752	856	2.627016
	28	159.25	276	91.02303	542	0.556452

29	833.9022	450	193.5247	1426	0.907258
30	746.4893	233	228.118	1408	0.469758
31	704.1155	944	250.4753	1743	1.903226
32	656.1885	435	175.6639	1363	0.877016
33	765.5405	222	224.9232	1623	0.447581
34	342.3613	357	156.6336	1017	0.719758
35	885	117	235.7799	1665	0.235887
36	799.2155	283	216.5134	1435	0.570565
37	777.9773	132	182.8619	1613	0.266129
38	695.1734	173	248.6615	1390	0.34879
39	857.3433	268	195.9306	1778	0.540323
40	681.644	455	193.4077	1578	0.917339
41	842.494	251	269.1292	1788	0.506048
42	656.0773	233	143.3936	1297	0.469758
43	691.8326	215	205.9691	1395	0.433468
44	196.3946	147	90.15182	752	0.296371
45	332.0782	294	93.97424	932	0.592742
46	387.1311	267	183.9309	984	0.538306
47	689.3929	196	149.9514	1385	0.395161
48	803.003	330	263.9694	1826	0.665323
49	797.1212	198	178.6902	1434	0.399194
50	674.8896	326	220.553	1392	0.657258
51	439.9953	430	182.0599	1239	0.866935
52	442.8077	1664	182.3552	1329	3.354839
53	715.3333	123	169.6589	1262	0.247984
54	172.6528	481	72.83796	741	0.969758
55	509.6335	322	212.6689	1408	0.649194
56	306.2206	281	96.19586	747	0.566532
57	940.7153	137	235.2323	1841	0.27621
58	1171.709	127	199.3282	1809	0.256048
59	669.9645	422	174.821	1617	0.850806
60	963.1716	134	226.1287	1722	0.270161
61	752.1073	177	177.4393	1614	0.356855
62	709.7563	554	159.0587	1600	1.116935
63	1382.232	69	214.2166	1952	0.139113
64	607.3707	348	219.4872	1407	0.701613
65	648.0417	216	245.5426	1634	0.435484
66	834.28	175	190.2023	1468	0.352823
67	642.8084	167	162.9637	1312	0.336694
68	826.9959	245	201.2949	1699	0.493952
69	1247.514	74	184.4236	1695	0.149194
70	758.7244	156	222.8217	1365	0.314516
71	611.879	124	261.9519	1523	0.25
72	700.5139	144	266.4752	1662	0.290323
73	677.5185	297	179.9858	1571	0.59879
74	859.9439	214	239.8926	1583	0.431452
75	770.3014	219	175.7918	1521	0.441532
76	669.8616	383	144.0618	1605	0.772177
77	713.1059	170	172.4138	1312	0.342742
78	790.2588	313	163.2198	1433	0.631048

79	758.8477	197	163.2099	1503	0.397177
80	634.4874	199	153.9439	1477	0.40121
81	662.3857	280	197.7231	1444	0.564516
82	718.445	200	211.9524	1750	0.403226
83	647.7824	942	181.6756	1643	1.899194
84	933.1013	316	162.1039	1810	0.637097
85	638.1471	238	174.0475	1228	0.479839
86	823.5439	239	155.1224	1317	0.481855
87	704.8432	185	189.2478	1555	0.372984
88	461.5356	407	183.1196	1107	0.820565
89	277.2583	5659	59.53367	971	11.40927
90	483.7554	2326	114.7216	1106	4.689516
91	266.5	702	109.6054	829	1.415323
92	627.3636	209	164.1949	1363	0.421371
93	650.405	242	186.137	1457	0.487903
94	721.6765	136	170.0778	1364	0.274194
95	185.3666	682	56.46384	670	1.375
96	173.0983	234	83.41434	573	0.471774
97	707.6688	154	269.297	1668	0.310484
98	315.7382	1421	80.33139	1084	2.864919
99	323.8061	686	110.167	920	1.383065
Total	461.8975	49600	274.6181	1952	100

Incremental "cube-based" algorithm validation clusters

V1	Mean	N	Std. Deviation	Maximum	% of Total N
0	1704.222	9	439.9749	2424	0.018182
1	1142.256	363	201.1516	2000	0.733333
2	303.7242	4743	52.09567	714	9.581818
3	223.423	4783	38.11789	633	9.662626
4	205.1127	559	86.6484	488	1.129293
5	196.9916	119	91.02677	556	0.240404
6	1365.122	237	220.5715	2063	0.478788
7	1565.506	164	194.005	2390	0.331313
8	1093.684	607	185.5263	1984	1.226263
9	1459.979	146	182.1741	2182	0.294949
10	558.695	659	139.913	1192	1.331313
11	1247.986	436	239.5901	2308	0.880808
12	1184.542	120	186.2341	1703	0.242424
13	192.9222	270	72.10823	665	0.545455
14	288.8857	210	139.2967	764	0.424242
15	1400.778	257	158.5177	2029	0.519192
16	1261.13	253	197.8712	1885	0.511111
17	193.0334	299	88.93814	667	0.60404
18	1418.575	106	200.2734	2258	0.214141
19	1336.339	177	151.4314	1806	0.357576
20	177.4115	520	72.39074	499	1.050505

21	209.5378	357	95.96718	602	0.721212
22	1202.1	290	226.5589	2061	0.585859
23	308.0373	1234	90.78058	892	2.492929
24	1431.511	90	205.9656	1971	0.181818
25	1246.842	19	137.862	1592	0.038384
26	198.7729	361	86.3844	780	0.729293
27	367.243	1362	93.47956	936	2.751515
28	173.7564	275	112.7126	627	0.555556
29	1035.118	510	198.172	1755	1.030303
30	1109.82	211	203.9309	1810	0.426263
31	1302.11	977	231.5398	2459	1.973737
32	953.1355	406	173.1769	1568	0.820202
33	1039.644	225	195.4258	1781	0.454545
34	455.9077	390	146.5001	1354	0.787879
35	1419.29	124	200.4909	2024	0.250505
36	1094.054	279	238.4082	2048	0.563636
37	1280.865	170	210.03	2197	0.343434
38	1249.736	140	215.8529	1876	0.282828
39	1435.407	268	172.6113	2296	0.541414
40	957.9191	408	174.6554	1641	0.824242
41	1417.183	235	207.0716	2220	0.474747
42	958.5964	223	144.8808	1928	0.450505
43	1016.855	193	208.8943	1728	0.389899
44	194.82	150	79.14349	609	0.30303
45	439.8229	288	125.7382	1042	0.581818
46	469.1745	298	165.4347	1074	0.60202
47	1300.55	171	163.6854	1970	0.345455
48	1390.709	313	263.7095	2497	0.632323
49	1263.314	210	196.9862	1935	0.424242
50	1241.54	302	198.8064	2076	0.610101
51	531.8853	436	177.4418	1455	0.880808
52	478.6262	1648	185.9295	1314	3.329293
53	1298.802	86	152.6666	1844	0.173737
54	175.5394	508	70.20416	609	1.026263
55	603.8886	359	182.075	1357	0.725253
56	392.5764	314	95.66162	968	0.634343
57	1467.19	142	196.4318	2372	0.286869
58	1626.685	89	213.9403	2460	0.179798
59	975.7596	391	186.6481	1709	0.789899
60	1505.312	125	231.7791	2116	0.252525
61	1304.349	192	163.4811	1946	0.387879
62	958.0371	539	147.2739	1686	1.088889
63	1841.387	62	221.4222	2555	0.125253
64	697.3696	349	199.5427	1520	0.705051
65	1183.785	205	218.7836	2040	0.414141
66	1252.657	236	201.5106	1963	0.476768
67	911.6957	161	155.4616	1444	0.325253
68	1363.702	262	202.5527	2343	0.529293
69	1783.4	55	207.5418	2196	0.111111
70	1299.167	144	301.2547	3309	0.290909

71	1187.957	115	212.6534	1852	0.232323
72	1090.729	155	264.6021	1894	0.313131
73	930.4244	311	172.1691	1770	0.628283
74	1262.571	196	217.1682	2081	0.39596
75	1175.228	237	211.8016	1906	0.478788
76	975.2868	380	147.9087	1703	0.767677
77	1320.92	137	195.4782	1971	0.276768
78	1340.373	306	157.7697	1934	0.618182
79	1302.727	183	144.9541	1783	0.369697
80	1252.804	138	128.6535	1651	0.278788
81	935.447	302	174.931	1526	0.610101
82	1039.868	219	240.3135	2225	0.442424
83	743.4807	984	206.3211	1817	1.987879
84	1477.957	301	144.4595	2205	0.608081
85	963.3812	223	195.8812	1764	0.450505
86	1009.4	215	167.3756	1889	0.434343
87	1326.568	146	182.8429	2015	0.294949
88	729.6339	366	165.7653	1403	0.739394
89	278.4205	5907	58.8463	670	11.93333
90	497.5281	2352	121.9731	1207	4.751515
91	336.154	695	116.2313	837	1.40404
92	881.981	211	170.8344	1732	0.426263
93	834.2355	259	230.4846	1503	0.523232
94	1265.93	142	178.8476	2091	0.286869
95	185.9723	723	58.47529	705	1.460606
96	165.1483	209	70.2278	555	0.422222
97	1019.553	161	292.3723	2227	0.325253
98	334.863	1423	80.63904	1194	2.874747
99	395.9401	685	122.1967	955	1.383838
Total	606.7363	49500	445.0818	3309	100

Appendix 2 – List of Variables in the Data Sets

In this Appendix we provide a list of all the variables in the three data files which were used in this study. The original variables appear in black color text and the transformations are marked in bold. The column "Uses in model" describes if and how the predictors are used in the model: 'Key' represents a unique key variable that is used as a reference in the scoring and in the output file. Variables marked as 'Y' are included in the model. Variables marked as "N" are not used in the model. Variables marked as 'T' denote a transformation of an original predictor that is used in the model instead of the original variable.

Name	Type	Description	Missing values	% Missing values	Position	Used in model
ACCNTNMB	Char	Donor ID	0	0.00%	01-09	key
TARGRESP	N1.0	Number of Fall 1995 Donation	0	0.00%	10	Y
TARGDOL	N4.0	Dollars of Fall 1995 Donation	0	0.00%	11-14	Y
ZIPCODE	Char	Zip	0	0.00%	15-19	N
SECANDIN	Y/N	2nd Address Indicator	0	0.00%	20	Y
STATCODE	Char	State	0	0.00%	21-22	Y
CHNGDATE	N6.0	Change of Address Date	0	0.00%	23-28	T
MEMBCODE	Char	Membership Code	0	0.00%	29	Y
RENTCODE	Char	Rental Exclusion Code, 'R' = Donor request for non-rental	0	0.00%	30	Y
PREFCODE	Char	Preferred Contributor Code (empty)	0	0.00%	31	N
CONTRFST	N3.0	First Contribution	0	0.00%	32-34	Y
DATEFST	yymm	First Contribution Date	0	0.00%	35-38	T
CONLARG	N4.0	Largest Contribution	0	0.00%	39-42	Y

229

Name	Type	Description	Missing values	% Missing values	Position	Used in model
DATELRG	yymm	Largest Contribution Date	0	0.00%	43-46	T
REINCODE	Char	Reinstate Code	0	0.00%	47	Y
REINDATE	yynndd	Reinstate Date	0	0.00%	48-53	T
NOCLBCOD	Char	No Club Contact Code {'B','C'}	0	0.00%	54	Y
NORETCOD	Char	No Return Postage Code 'N' = Donor request of no.	0	0.00%	55	Y
NOSUSCOD	Char	No Sustain Fund Code, 'F' = Donor request of no	0	0.00%	56	Y
NONPRCOD	char	No Premium Contact Code 'S' = Donor request of no.	0	0.00%	57	Y
FIRMCOD	Char	'01' = Firm, '02' = Head of HH code	0	0.00%	58-59	Y
SEX		Gender: {'B'= Both, 'C'= Company, 'F'= Female, 'M'= Male, 'U'= Unknown.}	0	0.00%	60	Y
CNTMLIF	N2.0	Time Contributed Lifetime	0	0.00%	61-62	Y
CNTRLIF	N4.0	Dollars Contributed Lifetime	0	0.00%	63-66	Y
SLTMLIF	N2.0	Time Solicitated Lifetime	0	0.00%	67-68	Y
CNDATE1	yymm	Latest Contribution Date	0	0.00%	69-72	T
CNDATE2	yymm	2nd Latest Contribution Date	59425	59.90%	73-76	T
CNDATE3	yymm	3rd Latest Contribution Date	67402	67.90%	77-80	T
CNDATE4	yymm	4th Latest Contribution Date	72264	72.80%	81-84	T
CNDATE5	yymm	5th Latest Contribution Date	75868	76.50%	85-88	T
CNDATE6	yymm	6th Latest Contribution Date	78779	79.40%	89-92	T
CNDATE7	yymm	7th Latest Contribution Date	81036	81.70%	93-96	T
CNDATE8	yymm	8th Latest Contribution Date	83022	83.70%	97-100	T
CNDATE9	yymm	9th Latest Contribution Date	84820	85.50%	101-104	T
CNDATE10	yymm	10th Latest Contribution Date	86851	87.60%	105-108	T
CNDOL1	N4.0	Latest contribution	0	0.00%	109-112	Y
CNDOL2	N3.0	2nd Latest Contribution	0	0.00%	113-115	Y
CNDOL3	N3.0	3rd Latest Contribution	0	0.00%	116-118	Y
CNDOL4	N3.0	4th Latest Contribution	0	0.00%	119-121	Y
CNDOL5	N3.0	5th Latest Contribution	0	0.00%	122-124	Y
CNDOL6	N3.0	6th Latest Contribution	0	0.00%	125-127	Y
CNDOL7	N3.0	7th Latest Contribution	0	0.00%	128-130	Y

Name	Type	Description	Missing values	% Missing values	Position	Used in model
CNDOL8	N3.0	8th Latest Contribution	0	0.00%	131-133	Y
CNDOL9	N3.0	9th Latest Contribution	0	0.00%	134-136	Y
CNDOL10	N3.0	10th Latest Contribution	0	0.00%	137-139	Y
SLDAT1	yymm	Latest Solicitation Date	0	0.00%	140-143	T
SLDAT2	yymm	2nd Latest Solicitation Date	24401	24.60%	144-147	T
SLDAT3	yymm	3rd Latest Solicitation Date	42018	42.40%	148-151	T
SLDAT4	yymm	4th Latest Solicitation Date	51165	51.60%	152-155	T
SLDAT5	yymm	5th Latest Solicitation Date	56352	56.80%	156-159	T
SLDAT6	yymm	6th Latest Solicitation Date	61392	61.90%	160-163	T
SLDAT7	yymm	7th Latest Solicitation Date	64947	65.50%	164-167	T
SLDAT8	yymm	8th Latest Solicitation Date	67045	67.60%	168-171	T
SLDAT9	yymm	9th Latest Solicitation Date	75243	75.80%	172-175	T
SLDAT10	yymm	10th Latest Solicitation Date	82642	83.30%	176-179	T
SLDAT11	yymm	11th Latest Solicitation Date	94604	95.40%	180-183	T
SLCOD1	Char	Latest Solicitation Code	0	0.00%	184-187	T
SLCOD2	Char	2nd Latest Solicitation Code	0	0.00%	188-191	T
SLCOD3	Char	3rd Latest Solicitation Code	0	0.00%	192-195	T
SLCOD4	Char	4th Latest Solicitation Code	0	0.00%	196-199	T
SLCOD5	Char	5th Latest Solicitation Code	0	0.00%	200-203	T
SLCOD6	Char	6th Latest Solicitation Code	0	0.00%	204-207	T
SLCOD7	Char	7th Latest Solicitation Code	0	0.00%	208-211	T
SLCOD8	Char	8th Latest Solicitation Code	0	0.00%	212-215	T
SLCOD9	Char	9th Latest Solicitation Code	0	0.00%	216-219	T
SLCOD10	Char	10th Latest Solicitation Code	0	0.00%	220-223	T
SLCOD11	Char	11th Latest Solicitation Code	0	0.00%	224-227	T
CNCOD1	Char	Latest Contribution Code	0	0.00%	228-231	T
CNCOD2	Char	2nd Latest Contribution Code	0	0.00%	232-235	T
CNCOD3	Char	3rd Latest Contribution Code	0	0.00%	236-239	T
CNCOD4	Char	4th Latest Contribution Code	0	0.00%	240-243	T

Name	Type	Description	Missing values	% Missing values	Position	Used in model
CNCOD5	Char	5th Latest Contribution Code	0	0.00%	244-247	T
CNCOD6	Char	6th Latest Contribution Code	0	0.00%	248-252	T
CNCOD7	Char	7th Latest Contribution Code	0	0.00%	253-257	T
CNCOD8	Char	8th Latest Contribution Code	0	0.00%	258-261	T
CNCOD9	Char	9th Latest Contribution Code	0	0.00%	262-265	T
CNCOD10	Char	10th Latest Contribution Code	0	0.00%	266-269	T
ADD_CHNG	Bool	'1'= address has changed prior to solicitation date (1-31/10/1999)	0	0.00%	270	Y
T_ADDCNG	N3.0	Months since last address change	0	0.00%	271-273	Y
MONTHFST	N3.0	Months since last contribution	0	0.00%	274-276	Y
MONTHLRG	N3.0	Months since Largest Contribution	0	0.00%	277-279	Y
REINMONT	N3.0	Months from reinstate {'0' for no reinstate}	0	0.00%	280-282	Y
CNTIME1	N3.0	Month since Latest Contribution	0	0.00%	283-285	Y
CNTIME2	N3.0	Month since 2nd Latest Contribution	59425	59.90%	286-288	N
CNTIME3	N3.0	Month since 3rd Latest Contribution	67402	67.90%	289-291	N
CNTIME4	N3.0	Month since 4th Latest Contribution	72264	72.80%	292-294	N
CNTIME5	N3.0	Month since 5th Latest Contribution	75868	76.50%	295-297	N
N_OF_CON	N2.0	Number of contributions	0	0.00%	298-299	Y
TOT_CONT	N4.0	Total Sum of 10 latest cont.	0	0.00%	300-303	Y
SLTIME1	N3.0	Months since Latest C127	0	0.00%	304-306	Y
SLTIME2	N3.0	Months since 2nd Latest Solicitation	24401	24.60%	307-309	N
SLTIME3	N3.0	Months since 3rd Latest Solicitation	42018	42.40%	310-312	N
SLTIME4	N3.0	Months since 4th Latest Solicitation	51165	51.60%	313-315	N
SLTIME5	N3.0	Months since 5th Latest Solicitation	56352	56.80%	316-318	N
SLTIME6	N3.0	Months since 6th Latest Solicitation	61392	61.90%	319-321	N
SLTIME7	N3.0	Months since 7th Latest Solicitation	64947	65.50%	322-324	N
SLTIME8	N3.0	Months since 8th Latest Solicitation	67045	67.60%	325-327	N
SLTIME9	N3.0	Months since 9th Latest Solicitation	75243	75.80%	328-330	N
SLTIME10	N3.0	Months since 10th Latest Solicitation	82642	83.30%	331-333	N
SLTIME11	N3.0	Months since 11th Latest Solicitation	94604	95.40%	334-336	N

Name	Type	Description	Missing values	% Missing values	Position	Used in model
N_OF_SOL	N2.0	Number of solicitations	0	0.00%	337-338	Y
CT1	Char	Latest contribution Type (Transformation from CNCOD1)	0	0.00%	339	Y
CT2	Char	2nd Latest contribution Type (Transformation from CNCOD2)	0	0.00%	340	Y
CT3	Char	3rd Latest contribution Type (Transformation from CNCOD3)	0	0.00%	341	Y
CT4	Char	4th Latest contribution Type (Transformation from CNCOD4)	0	0.00%	342	Y
CT5	Char	5th Latest contribution Type (Transformation from CNCOD5)	0	0.00%	343	Y
CT6	Char	6th Latest contribution Type (Transformation from CNCOD6)	0	0.00%	344	Y
CT7	Char	7th Latest contribution Type (Transformation from CNCOD7)	0	0.00%	345	Y
CT8	Char	8th Latest contribution Type (Transformation from CNCOD8)	0	0.00%	346	Y
CT9	Char	9th Latest contribution Type (Transformation from CNCOD9)	0	0.00%	347	Y
CT10	Char	10th Latest contribution Type (Transformation from CNCOD10)	0	0.00%	348	Y
TYPE_A	N2.0	Number of type A contributions	0	0.00%	349-350	Y
TYPE_B	N2.0	Number of type B contributions	0	0.00%	351-352	Y
TYPE_C	N2.0	Number of type C contributions	0	0.00%	353-354	Y
TYPE_M	N2.0	Number of type M contributions	0	0.00%	355-356	Y
TYPE_O	N2.0	Number of Other types contributions	0	0.00%	357-358	Y
ST1	Char	Latest Solicitation Type (Transformation from SLCOD1)	0	0.00%	359	Y
ST2	Char	2nd Latest Solicitation Type (Transformation from SLCOD2)	0	0.00%	360	Y
ST3	Char	3rd Latest Solicitation Type (Transformation from SLCOD3)	0	0.00%	361	Y
ST4	Char	4th Latest Solicitation Type (Transformation from SLCOD4)	0	0.00%	362	Y
ST5	Char	5th Latest Solicitation Type (Transformation from SLCOD5)	0	0.00%	363	Y
ST6	Char	6th Latest Solicitation Type (Transformation from SLCOD6)	0	0.00%	364	Y
ST7	Char	7th Latest Solicitation Type (Transformation from SLCOD7)	0	0.00%	365	Y
ST8	Char	8th Latest Solicitation Type (Transformation from SLCOD8)	0	0.00%	366	Y
ST9	Char	9th Latest Solicitation Type (Transformation from SLCOD9)	0	0.00%	367	Y
ST10	Char	10th Latest Solicitation Type (Transformation from SLCOD10)	0	0.00%	368	Y
SLTYPE_A	N2.0	Number of Solicitation type A	0	0.00%	369-370	Y
SLTYPE_B	N2.0	Number of Solicitation type B	0	0.00%	371-372	Y
SLTYPE_C	N2.0	Number of type Solicitation C	0	0.00%	373-374	Y

Name	Type	Description	Missing values	% Missing values	Position	Used in model
SLTYPE_M	N2.0	Number of type Solicitation M	0	0.00%	375-376	Y
SLTYPE_O	N2.0	Number of Other type Solicitation	0	0.00%	377-378	Y
ZIP2DIG	Char 2	Zip code two digits	0	0.00%	379-380	Y

Appendix 3 – The effect of using the cubes (details)

The details result of comparing the original training dataset to the "cube" training dataset are:

(Limited to attributes where the difference average is larger then 0 or the difference STD is larger the 0)

Variable	Training Dataset				Training dataset converted into cubes				Difference	
	Min	Max	Avg.	Std.	Min	Max	Avg.	Std.	Avg.	Std.
Donor ID	0	3	0.26	0.44	0	3	0.20	0.40	0.06	0.04
Gender	0	250	0.00	0.01	0	250	0.00	0.01	0.00	0.00
Dollars Contributed Lifetime – quartile 2	0	500	7.97	6.76	0	500	4.87	7.71	3.10	0.95
3rd Latest Contribution Date - quartile 3	0	40	4.04	5.89	0	40	1.80	5.05	2.24	0.84
3rd Latest Contribution Date – quartile 4	0	2175	33.62	68.57	0	2175	30.19	68.64	3.43	0.07
4th Latest Contribution Date – quartile 1	0	60	8.87	10.95	0	60	5.73	10.40	3.14	0.54
4th Latest Contribution Date – quartile 2	0	250	9.32	8.19	0	250	6.11	9.19	3.21	1.00
4th Latest Contribution Date – quartile 3	0	300	3.79	7.62	0	300	2.54	7.27	1.25	0.35
4th Latest Contribution Date – quartile 4	0	250	2.91	6.75	0	250	1.91	6.34	1.00	0.41
5th Latest Contribution Date – quartile 1	0	200	2.38	6.08	0	200	1.54	5.67	0.84	0.41

5th Latest Contribution Date – quartile 2	0	200	2.02	5.61	0	200	1.28	5.19	0.74	0.42
5th Latest Contribution Date – quartile 3	0	200	1.72	5.19	0	200	1.07	4.76	0.65	0.43
5th Latest Contribution Date – quartile 4	0	200	1.52	5.06	0	200	0.95	4.69	0.57	0.37
6th Latest Contribution Date – quartile 1	0	200	1.31	4.55	0	200	0.79	4.16	0.52	0.39
6th Latest Contribution Date – quartile 2	0	200	1.17	4.53	0	200	0.70	4.17	0.47	0.36
6th Latest Contribution Date – quartile 3	0	200	0.95	3.92	0	200	0.55	3.56	0.40	0.36
7th Latest Contribution Date – quartile 1	0	120	7.84	20.94	0	120	6.88	19.84	0.96	1.10
7th Latest Contribution Date – quartile 2	0	167	39.31	46.31	0	167	34.80	47.45	4.51	1.14
7th Latest Contribution Date – quartile 3	0	166	20.93	22.87	0	166	16.22	23.24	4.71	0.38
7th Latest Contribution Date – quartile 4	0	107	1.23	7.24	0	107	1.01	6.57	0.22	0.67
8th Latest Contribution Date – quartile 1	0	130	13.02	10.78	0	130	8.29	11.32	4.73	0.54
8th Latest Contribution Date – quartile 2	0	2000	3.08	3.25	0	2000	3.08	3.25	0.00	0.00
8th Latest Contribution	0	79	27.10	46.63	0	79	23.73	46.85	3.37	0.22

236

Date – quartile 3										
8th Latest Contribution Date – quartile 4	0	3	6.79	1.31	0	3	0.14	1.50	6.65	0.19
9th Latest Contribution Date – quartile 1	0	250	4.75	3.49	0	250	4.75	3.49	0.00	0.00

Table 46 : Detailed cube effect on the DMEF dataset

The total difference in the mean of the attributes (between the original data and the cubes data) is 47.83, so the average mean deviation per attribute is 0.15

The total difference in the standard deviation of the attributes is 11.29, so the average STD deviation per attribute is 0.036.

The summary of the results for the mean is:

Mean Deviation	# of attributes
0	284
0.5	5
1	7
1.4	2
2	0
2.5	1
3	0
3.5	5
> 3.5	4

Table 47 : Means deviation due to the cubes

This table shows that for 284 attributes there is no difference in the mean when the cubes are used, for 5 attributes the difference in the mean when the cubes are used is 0.5, etc.

The summary of the results for the STD is:

STD Deviation	# of attributes
0	284
0.5	16
1	6
1.4	2
2	0
2.5	0
3	0
3.5	0
> 3.5	0

Table 48 : STD deviation due to the cubes

This table shows that for 284 attributes there is no difference in the STD when the cubes are used and not the original data, for 16 attributes the difference in the STD when the cubes are used is 0.5, etc.

www.ingramcontent.com/pod-product-compliance
Lightning Source LLC
LaVergne TN
LVHW042332060326
832902LV00006B/131